W9-ACB-838

Race Relations

Abortion

Drug & Alcohol Abuse

Health Care

Immigration

Marriage & Family Issues

Obesity

Race Relations

Technology

Race Relations

Hal Marcovitz

The opinions and conclusions expressed by the author are not necessarily representative of the Gallup Organization or its subsidiaries.

Produced by OTTN Publishing, Stockton, New Jersey

Mason Crest Publishers
370 Reed Road
Broomall, PA 19008
www.masoncrest.com

Printed and bound in Malaysia.

First printing

1 3 5 7 9 8 6 4 2

Library of Congress Cataloging-in-Publication Data

Marcovitz, Hal.
Race relations / Hal Marcovitz.
p. cm. — (Gallup major trends and events)
Includes bibliographical references and index.
ISBN-13: 978-1-59084-968-2 (hard cover)
ISBN-10: 1-59084-968-X (hard cover)
1. United States—Race relations—Juvenile literature. 2. United States—Ethnic relations—Juvenile literature. 3. Minorities—United States—Juvenile literature. 4. United States—Social conditions—Juvenile literature. I. Title. II. Series.
E184.A1M295 2006
305.8'00973—dc22

2005016299

TABLE OF CONTENTS

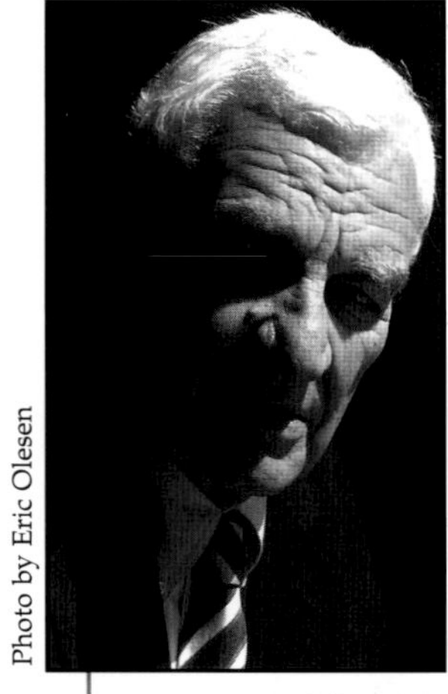
Photo by Eric Olesen

Introduction

By Alec Gallup, Chairman, The Gallup Poll

In ways both obvious and subtle, the United States of today differs significantly from the United States that existed at the turn of the 20th century. In 1900, for example, America had not yet taken its place among the world's most influential nations; today the United States stands by itself as the globe's lone superpower. The 1900 census counted about 76 million Americans, largely drawn from white European peoples such as the English, Irish, and Germans; 100 years later the U.S. population was approaching 300 million, and one in every eight residents was of Hispanic origin. In the first years of the 20th century, American society offered women few opportunities to pursue professional careers, and, in fact, women had not yet gained the right to vote. Though slavery had been abolished, black Americans 100 years ago continued to be treated as second-class citizens, particularly in the South, where the Jim Crow laws that would endure for another half-century kept the races separate and unequal.

The physical texture and the pace of American life, too, were much different 100 years ago—or, for that matter, even 50 years ago. Accelerating technological and scientific progress, a hallmark of modern times, has made possible a host of innovations that Americans today take for granted but that would have been unimaginable three generations ago—from brain scans to microwave ovens to cell phones, laptop computers, and the Internet.

No less important than the material, social, and political changes the United States has witnessed over the past century are the changes in American attitudes and perceptions. For example, the way Americans relate to their government and their fellow citizens, how they view marriage and child-rearing norms, where they set the boundary between society's responsibilities and the individual's rights and freedoms—all are key components of Americans' evolving understanding of their nation and its place in the world.

The books in this series examine important issues that have perennially concerned (and sometimes confounded) Americans since the turn of the 20th century. Each volume draws on an array of sources to provide vivid detail and historical context. But, as suggested by the series title, GALLUP MAJOR TRENDS AND EVENTS: THE PULSE OF OUR NATION, 1900 TO THE PRESENT, these books make particular use of the Gallup Organization's vast archive of polling data.

There is perhaps no better source for tracking and understanding American public opinion than Gallup, a name that has been synonymous with opinion polling for seven decades. Over the years, Gallup has elicited responses from more than 3.5 million people on more than 125,000 questions. In 1936 the organization, then known as the American Institute of Public Opinion, emerged into the spotlight when it correctly predicted that Franklin Roosevelt would be reelected president of the United States. This directly contradicted the well-respected Literary Digest Poll, which had announced that Alfred Landon, governor of Kansas, would not only become president but would win in a landslide. Since then Gallup polls have not simply been a fixture in election polling and analysis; they have also cast light on public opinion regarding a broad variety of social, economic, and cultural issues.

Polling results tend to be most noticed during political campaigns or in the wake of important events; during these times, polling provides snapshots of public opinion. This series, however, is more concerned with long-term attitude trends than with responses to breaking news. Thus data from many years of Gallup polls are used to trace the evolution of American attitudes. How, for example, have Americans historically viewed immigration? Did attitudes toward foreign newcomers shift during the Great Depression, after the 1941 Japanese attack on Pearl Harbor, or after the terrorist attacks of September 11, 2001? Do opinions on immigration vary across different age, gender, and ethnic groups?

Or, taking another particularly divisive issue treated in this series, what did Americans think about abortion during the many decades the procedure was generally illegal? How has public opinion changed since the Supreme Court's landmark 1973 *Roe v. Wade* decision? How many Americans now favor overturning *Roe*?

By understanding where we as a society have been, we can better understand where we are—and, sometimes, where we are going.

1 LANCING THE BOIL OF RACISM

Senate Majority Leader Trent Lott, standing next to President George W. Bush, applauds U.S. Senator Strom Thurmond (seated) during a December 2002 party. Racially insensitive remarks made by Lott during the celebration ultimately resulted in the Mississippi senator stepping down from his leadership position.

In 2002, U.S. Senator Strom Thurmond celebrated his 100th birthday—an amazing accomplishment for anyone, let alone for someone in a position of great political power. While Thurmond was hardly the firebrand he had been in his younger years, the fact that he celebrated this birthday as a member of the U.S. Senate reflected his enduring popularity with the voters of South Carolina.

Still, his 100th birthday party on December 5 also happened to be his retirement party. Confined to a wheelchair and falling victim to the infirmities of advanced age, Strom Thurmond was finally relinquishing his seat.

Many friends and political allies attended the senator's retirement party, including Senator Trent Lott, a Republican from Mississippi. Lott was the majority leader of the Senate, meaning he held the top party post in the lawmaking chamber. As majority leader, he held enormous influence over the direction of the federal government as well as over the legislation brought to the floor of the Senate for consideration.

During Thurmond's retirement party, Lott made a short speech. In his remarks, Lott recalled that in 1948, when Thurmond was serving as governor of South Carolina, he had made an unsuccessful run for the presidency. "I want to say this about my state," Lott told the crowd. "When Strom Thurmond ran for president we voted for him. We're proud of it. And if the rest of the country had followed our lead, we wouldn't have had all these problems over all these years, either."

INSENSITIVE AND OFFENSIVE REMARKS

Lott's comments may have been intended as a warm farewell for an old friend, but they touched off a firestorm of protest. In 1948, Strom Thurmond was an ardent proponent of segregation. His campaign for the presidency was sparked by President Harry Truman's decision to include a civil rights plank in the 1948 Democratic Party platform. At the time, Thurmond was a Democrat, but when the plank was approved at the party convention that summer, the governor stormed out of the meeting hall, formed his own party (the States' Rights Party), and commenced a campaign for the presidency based on segregation of the races: he opposed blacks and whites attending the same schools, eating in the same restaurants, riding on the same railroad cars, and enjoying movies or other entertainment in the same theaters. During the campaign, Thurmond said, "All the laws of Washington and all the bayonets of the Army cannot force the Negro into our homes, our schools, our churches."

The States' Rights Party candidate fell far short of winning the White House, however. Thurmond won just four states in 1948: South Carolina, Louisiana, Alabama, and Trent Lott's state of Mississippi.

Within hours of Thurmond's retirement party, many black political leaders, civil rights leaders, and other national figures denounced Lott's comment. "It sends a chilling message to all people," warned U.S. Representative Elijah Cummings of Maryland, the chairman of the Congressional Black Caucus. "These are the kinds of words that tear this nation apart." Similarly, U.S. Representative John Lewis of Georgia said,

> I could not believe he was saying what he said. . . . Was he saying Jim Crow should still be the law of the land in the Deep South? Should we still have segregated schools and signs that read, 'White waiting, Colored waiting, White men, Colored men, White women, Colored women?' Would America be better off without

the Civil Rights Act of 1964, the Voting Rights Act of 1965, the fair housing act or the equal employment act? . . . It is frightening, unbelievable and unacceptable that an elected official, the . . . leader of the U.S. Senate, would make a statement condoning a period of history burdened by overt racism, violence, fear and oppression.

GROWING MINORITY POPULATION

Trent Lott's words were distressing to many people because, quite simply, the United States is a country of many races. White people make up a significant majority of the population—according to the 2000 U.S. census, about 211 million of the nation's 281 million people are white. Nevertheless, that still leaves some 70 million people who are members of other races. In fact, the minority population of the United States has grown dramatically over the years, and statistics indicate that

A Hispanic family prepares to cross a street in Chicago's Little Village neighborhood. According to recent figures from the U.S. Census Bureau, Hispanics are now the largest minority group in the United States.

it is projected to grow further as the 21st century progresses.

In 2003, the Census Bureau reported that in California, Hawaii, New Mexico, and Washington, D.C., the minority populations outnumber the white population. That same year the Census Bureau reported that Hispanics—who can be either white or black, but are nonetheless considered a separate minority group—had passed African Americans as the largest minority group in the United States, with some 37 million members. Blacks numbered about 36 million in that year. Both of these ethnic groups have grown in recent years—the number of blacks increased by about 1.5 percent while the number of Hispanics grew by 4.7 percent from 2000 to 2003. The Asian population in the United States has also grown tremendously in recent years. During the 1990s, this group grew by 43 percent, and by 2002, the number of Asians living in the United States was recorded at 12.5 million.

Larry Sink, a U.S. Census Bureau analyst, explained to a CNN reporter that Asian and Hispanic growth is "largely being fueled by immigration." Asians and Hispanics want to come to the United States in the 21st century for the same reason Europeans flocked to these shores in the 19th century: America is seen as the land of freedom, jobs, and equal opportunity. The CNN story also quoted John Haaga, an analyst for the Washington-based Population Reference Bureau, as saying that Nevada, Georgia, and North Carolina showed the greatest minority population growth. This influx is "largely a condition of jobs and the network of people they know there," he said. "That's the traditional American experience."

Many other races are represented in the United States: American Indians, Alaska Natives, Hawaiians, Pacific Islanders, Arabs, and others. In all cases, the minority populations of the United States have grown in recent years.

And so when Trent Lott wondered aloud what life would have been like had Strom Thurmond won the presidency in 1948 with his segregationist ideas, it is understandable that many people were distressed by his remarks.

POOR CHOICE OF WORDS

Shortly after Lott's remarks were publicized, the Gallup Organization, which conducts national public-opinion polls on important issues, asked Americans what they thought of the senator's statement. According to the poll, 62 percent of the respondents thought "Lott made a poor choice of words and did not mean to endorse segregationist policies," while 30 percent of respondents thought "Lott really believes the country would have been better off if it elected a president in 1948 who endorsed segregationist policies." In other words, a majority of Americans were willing to give the senator the benefit of the doubt when he said he did not mean to endorse segregation. However, a significant number of people took his words differently.

The people most disturbed by the majority leader's statement were members of minority groups. A few days after the initial poll, the Gallup Organization conducted a second poll, questioning blacks on the Lott issue. Among the 135 African Americans polled, only 31 percent believed Lott simply had made a poor choice of words, while 63 percent believed the senator meant what he had said.

During the next few days, the press started examining Trent Lott's record on civil rights. Over the course of his long career in Congress, the Mississippi Republican had opposed the use of busing to desegregate schools, backed tax breaks for private schools that exclude black students, and had even submitted a brief to the U.S. Supreme Court arguing that "racial discrimination does not always violate public policy." He also had opposed the extension of the Voting Rights Act and opposed the

Opinions of the Lott/Thurmond Controversy

"Based on what you have heard or read, do you think that Senator Lott really believes the country would have been better off if it elected a president in 1948 who endorsed segregationist policies, or do you think Lott made a poor choice of words and did not mean to endorse segregationist policies?"

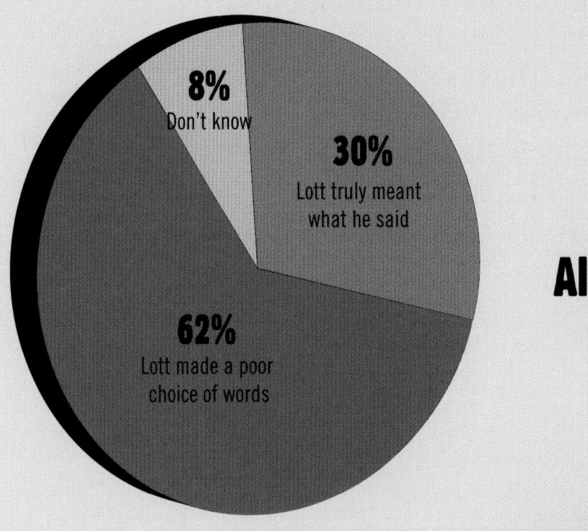

All Respondents

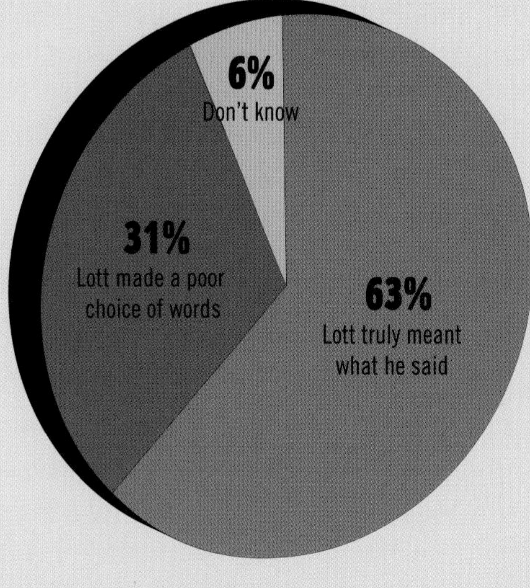

Polls taken December 2002; 1,009 and 135 total respondents
Source: The Gallup Organization

designation of a national holiday to honor slain civil rights leader Martin Luther King Jr.—a holiday that even Strom Thurmond had supported.

Lott apologized for the remarks he had made at Thurmond's retirement party, but his words doomed his leadership position. Under pressure from President George W. Bush as well as other Republican leaders, Lott resigned as Senate majority leader, although he continued to represent his state in the Senate. In a speech made a short time after Thurmond's retirement party, Bush said, "Recent comments by Senator Lott do not reflect the spirit of our country." Just before the speech, Bush had told his aides that he had to speak out against Lott's remarks. "This is going to be painful. But we have to do it. It's like lancing a boil."

2

THE PATH TO DESEGREGATION

Marian Anderson was one of America's most gifted opera singers. Born in 1902 in Philadelphia, she learned to sing in the choir of the Union Baptist Church, where she developed her incredible contralto voice. By the time she was 16 years old, Anderson was singing to sold-out audiences in New York City as well as in European capitals.

In 1939, Anderson agreed to perform in Washington, D.C., at a benefit concert for Howard University, a college for black students. Over the years, Anderson had performed three benefit concerts for the university before small crowds, but for the 1939 event the university decided a larger concert hall would be more appropriate. Officials sponsoring the benefit concert approached the Daughters of the American Revolution (DAR), the organization that owns the 2,000-seat Constitution Hall in Washington, D.C. Mrs. Henry M. Robert Jr., president of the DAR, delivered the organization's response to Howard University: Marian Anderson would not be permitted to sing in

(Opposite) Eleanor Roosevelt presents an award to Marian Anderson, circa 1939. The First Lady resigned from the prestigious DAR after that organization refused to permit Anderson to perform in Constitution Hall because she was black. Gallup polls found that a majority of Americans supported Roosevelt's decision.

Constitution Hall. The reason? Marian Anderson is a Negro, and Negroes were not welcome there.

While today there are laws that prohibit racial discrimination, in 1939 such discrimination was common. This was especially true in the South, where the so-called Jim Crow laws remained very much in effect. As a result, blacks and other minorities were banned from whites-only restaurants, theaters, swimming pools, and schools. Washington, D.C., may be the nation's capital, but it is also a southern city, situated between the states of Maryland and Virginia. In Washington, blacks were banned from many places. One of those places was Constitution Hall.

The DAR's decision to bar Anderson from Constitution Hall led one of the organization's most prominent members to resign. That member was Eleanor Roosevelt, the first lady of the United States. In a letter to Mrs. Robert, the first lady wrote:

> I am afraid that I have never been a very useful member of the Daughters of the American Revolution, so I know it will make very little difference to you whether I resign, or whether I continue to be a member of your organization.
>
> However, I am in complete disagreement with the attitude taken in refusing Constitution Hall to a great artist. You have set an example which seems to me unfortunate, and I feel obliged to send in to you my resignation. You had an opportunity to lead in an enlightened way and it seems to me that your organization has failed.
>
> I realize that many people will not agree with me, but feeling as I do this seems to me the only proper procedure to follow.

Mrs. Roosevelt was wrong about people's perspectives—as it turned out, many people did agree with her. A Gallup poll taken shortly after the first lady resigned from the DAR found a large majority of Americans supporting her decision. Nearly 60 percent of respondents

An enormous crowd enjoys the performance by opera singer Marian Anderson at the Lincoln Memorial in April 1939. Although Anderson was widely considered one of the greatest singers of her day, she faced racial discrimination throughout her career.

backed her, while just 28 percent indicated they thought she was wrong.

Mrs. Roosevelt did more than just resign from the DAR. She asked Harold Ickes, the Secretary of the Interior, to make the Lincoln Memorial available for an open-air concert that would feature Anderson. Ickes, who had the support of President Franklin D. Roosevelt, agreed, and on April 9, 1939, some 75,000 people gathered in front of the memorial to hear a concert by the famed opera star. Ickes himself introduced Anderson to the crowd: "Genius, like Justice, is blind. . . . Genius draws no color line. She has endowed Marian Anderson with such a voice as lifts any individual above his fellows and is a matter of exultant pride to any race."

A HISTORY OF PREJUDICE

Marian Anderson's concert marked an important moment in American race relations. Yet the actions of the first lady and president regarding the concert mark one of the few times in the first half of the 20th century that national leaders attempted to build a bridge between the races. The first half of the 20th century was a time of discrimination, prejudice, and outright hatred toward minorities.

Changes to the Constitution after the Civil War ended in 1865 had abolished slavery and officially given black Americans legal rights equal to those of whites. However, in the decades after the Civil War, the rights of blacks were eroded—gradually in some places, more quickly in others. In 1896 the U.S. Supreme Court ruled in *Plessy v. Ferguson* that blacks could be excluded from whites-only schools, railroad cars, theaters, and other places as long as the facilities available to them were equal to whites' facilities. The concept is known as "separate but equal." In truth, however, although schools and other facilities for black were separate, they were rarely equal.

For blacks in the South, the euphoria of emancipation after the Civil War was dampened by the harsh realities of Reconstruction. During this time, African Americans were allowed to vote and hold public office, and many blacks were elected to state legislatures and even Congress. Still, white-dominated state legislatures in the South passed laws limiting the rights of blacks. The U.S. Congress responded by adopting several acts protecting the civil rights of blacks. To enforce the laws, the president maintained a force of Union soldiers in the South—a fact of life that made most southern whites seethe with hate.

The 1876 presidential election ended in a virtual dead heat between Rutherford B. Hayes and Samuel Tilden. Tilden won the popular vote, but each candidate was short of the required number of votes in the Electoral College to win the White House. Hayes broke the deadlock when he lured electoral votes from the Southern states by agreeing to withdraw federal troops.

An African-American man uses the back door to enter a theater in a Mississippi city, circa 1939. Because of so-called "Jim Crow laws" throughout the South, blacks were often either barred from entering restaurants, theaters, and other public places, or they were forced to use separate entrances and sit in specially marked sections away from white customers.

With no troops to protect black citizens or enforce the federal civil rights laws, it didn't take long for minority rights to erode in the South once again.

It was during this period that the states in the South passed the so-called Jim Crow laws, which limited blacks' access to schools, railroad cars, and other places. "Jim Crow" was a mythical character created by the white performer Thomas Rice, who entertained his audiences by wearing black face makeup and portraying a black man as ignorant, lazy, and subservient. Across the South, the Jim Crow laws were designed to separate blacks and whites. Here is how black writer W.E.B. DuBois described riding in a railroad car reserved for blacks:

> The "Jim-Crow" car is caked with dirt, the floor is gummy and the windows dirty. The conductor gruffly

asks for your tickets. Lunch rooms either "don't serve niggers" or serve them at some dirty and ill-attended hole-in-the-wall. Toilet rooms are often filthy.

Lynchings were also common at the time. Gangs of whites riding under the cover of night would find a lone black man along a secluded road and then kidnap and murder him by hanging the hapless victim from a tree. Usually, the unfortunate individual would be left hanging so that other blacks could see what fate awaited them. Between 1889 and 1918, it was estimated that whites lynched more than 2,500 blacks in the South. Fifty of the victims were women. Often, the person who was lynched had done nothing to provoke the attack. The white journalist H.L. Mencken wrote, "In sheer high spirits, some convenient African is taken at random and lynched, as the newspapers say, 'on general principles.'"

Members of the Ku Klux Klan parade down a street in Washington, D.C. during a 1926 rally. For decades Klansmen terrorized and intimidated black Americans who dared to register to vote in the South or protest against discriminatory laws.

Many of the lynchings were undoubtedly committed by members of the Ku Klux Klan, an organization formed following the Civil War. The group takes its name from the Greek word *kyklos*, which means "circle." Klansmen wear white robes and hide their identities by wearing masks and high, pointed hats.

While the Ku Klux Klan is nothing more than an organization of racists and terrorists, the group received a sizable measure of credibility in 1915 with the release of the film *Birth of a Nation*. Directed by pioneering filmmaker D.W. Griffith, the silent movie dramatizes life in the South during the Civil War and Reconstruction. The film portrays blacks as corrupt and evil while showing the Ku Klux Klan as a heroic organization, its members riding to the aid of white women threatened by black rapists. President Woodrow Wilson saw the film at a special White House screening and said afterwards, "It is like writing history with lightning, and my only regret is that it is all so terribly true." The film played in sold-out theaters, despite the protest by black civil rights activists that it was full of lies.

"TRICKY AND CUNNING"

Blacks were not the only minority members to suffer discrimination in the United States. The Chinese, Japanese, Hispanics, and others often have been targets as well. The first Chinese immigrants arrived in California in 1849, drawn to the United States to escape poverty, famine, war, and a repressive government back home. These immigrants were so certain they would have a good life in California that they called California *Gum San*, which means "Gold Mountain." They found jobs as farm workers and laborers; many constructed the first western railroads.

During the gold rush, some Chinese mined for gold on their own or worked in white-owned mines, but many others found ways to make their living in the bustling city of San Francisco by opening laundries, restaurants, and other businesses. Meanwhile, many Chinese immigrants continued to work in the fields on the sprawling California fruit farms. Although using a term for Chinese immigrants that would today be regarded as derogatory, the writer Mark Twain found many reasons to admire the Chinese. In his book *Roughing It* (1871), he wrote:

> They are quiet, peaceable, tractable, free from drunkenness, and they are as industrious as the day is long. A disorderly Chinaman is rare, and a lazy one does not exist. So long as a Chinaman has strength to use his hands he needs no support from anybody; white men often complain of want of work, but a Chinaman offers no such

This 1881 cartoon represents the discriminatory attitudes that many Americans expressed toward Chinese immigrants. The cartoon attributes a number of social problems, including immorality, disease, filth, and the ruin of "white labor," to the Chinese.

complaint; he always manages to find something to do.

Once the gold rush ended and the transcontinental railroad was completed, however, the Chinese became the focus of intense racial hatred by white Californians. Although during the boom times, whites had been content to let Chinese workers perform the most menial and disagreeable jobs, when employment became scarce, whites demanded that they be given preference for the jobs over the Chinese.

Anti-Chinese attitudes were not limited to California. In 1882, the U.S. Congress passed the Chinese Exclusion Act, which limited Chinese immigration to people with mothers and fathers already living in the United States. Over the years, the Chinese Exclusion Act would be extended several times; it was not repealed until World War II, a time when China was an ally of the United States and when sympathy for Chinese immigrants—many of whom were fleeing their homes because of a brutal Japanese invasion and occupation of China—was high.

Still, during most of the first half of the twentieth century, prejudice against the Chinese was widespread. Just as blacks were victims of lynchings, Chinese immigrants fell victim to angry whites as well. Twain described one such instance in *Roughing It*: "As I write, news comes that in broad daylight in San Francisco, some boys have stoned an inoffensive Chinaman to death, and that although a large crowd witnessed the shameful deed, no one interfered."

While Congress slowed Chinese immigration, Japanese immigration increased. Indeed, with a labor pool of immigrant Chinese no longer available to them, the California fruit growers were desperate for a cheap source of workers. By the early 1900s, Japanese immigrants were arriving in the United States in large numbers, and they took the jobs in the fields. The Japanese proved to be much shrewder than their Chinese predecessors, however. At first, they worked for cheap wages—just thirty or forty cents a day—but once they had monopolized the farm jobs, they demanded higher wages. The fruit growers had no choice but to pay the Japanese what they wanted. "Japanese labor is not cheap labor," fumed an editorial writer at the *Los Angeles Times*. "The little brown traders know how to get as much for their product as the traffic will bear."

In 1907, members of the California Fruit Growers Convention, longing for the days of cheap Chinese labor, wrote in a report:

> The Chinese when they were here were ideal. They were patient, plodding and uncomplaining in the performance of a most menial service. They submitted to anything, never violating a contract. The Japanese now coming in are a tricky and cunning lot, who break contracts and become quite independent. They are not organized into unions, but their clannishness seems to operate as a union would. One trick is to contract work at a certain price and then in the rush of the harvest season to strike unless wages are raised.

In 1913, the California Legislature adopted the Alien Land Bill, which barred Japanese Americans from leasing land and from passing land they already owned to their heirs.

In the following years, hostility between Japan and the United States escalated as the Japanese government, controlled by the military, sought to dominate Asia. Japan invaded Manchuria in 1933 and declared war on China in 1937, resulting in a brutal occupation. In Tokyo, Japanese leaders ignored U.S. demands that it withdraw from China. Instead, the Japanese secretly prepared for war against the United States. They started that war on December 7, 1941, when Japanese forces attacked Pearl Harbor.

In the months before the attack, Americans had become more and more wary of the Japanese. In 1940, a Gallup poll asked, "Do you think the increase of Japan's power in the Far East is at present a serious threat to the United States?" Nearly 50 percent of the respondents thought it was.

Following the Japanese surprise attack on Pearl Harbor, U.S. authorities feared that Japanese Americans living on the West Coast would work as spies or saboteurs against the United States. On February 2, 1942, President Franklin D. Roosevelt signed Executive Order 9066, authorizing the internment of some 110,000 Japanese immigrants for the duration of the war. Some two-thirds of the immigrants taken into custody were American citizens; over half were children.

ZOOT SUIT RIOTS

The war years were also difficult for Hispanics living in the United States. Immigrants from Mexico who settled in California found themselves the victims of prejudice from the white majority. Many young Mexican Americans enjoyed wearing flashy clothes—long jackets and wide-brimmed hats known as "zoot suits." By 1943, tensions between whites and "zoot-suiters" had escalated. On the night of June 3, there were a couple of minor fights between whites and Hispanic zoot-suiters. Four days later, the "Zoot Suit Riots" erupted in Los Angeles, in which thousands of white servicemen and civilians fanned out in the city in search of Hispanic youths to attack. As for the police, they proved to be willing accomplices to the white rioters. The chaos lasted three days. One eyewitness was Al Waxman, editor of the *Eastside Journal*, a Los Angeles newspaper. He wrote:

> At Twelfth and Central I came upon a scene that will long live in my memory. . . . Four boys came out of a

> pool hall. They were wearing the zoot suits that have become the symbol of a fighting flag. Police ordered them into arrest cars. One refused. He asked, "Why am I being arrested?" The police officer answered with three swift blows of the night-stick across the boy's head and he went down. As he sprawled, he was kicked in the face. Police had difficulty loading his body into the vehicle because he was one-legged and wore a wooden limb. . . .
>
> At the next corner a Mexican mother cried out, "Don't take my boy, he did nothing. He's only fifteen years old. Don't take him." She was struck across the jaw with a night-stick and almost dropped that two-and-a-half year old baby that was clinging in her arms.

SOME SUCCEEDED DESPITE RACISM

The prejudice, intimidation, and hatred of the Zoot Suit Riots were directed at Hispanics who had done nothing wrong. They, like other minority members, contributed to society, and, if given the chance, they could prove themselves capable of achieving great things. Marian Anderson is certainly an example of a young black person with talent and the will to succeed. Another is Booker T. Washington, who had been born a slave, but achieved many accomplishments, among them founding a school in the early years of the 20th century that later would become Tuskegee University. By the time Washington died in 1915, while making a speech in support of civil rights, Tuskegee had 1,500 students, a faculty of 180, and an endowment of $2 million.

In sports, Jack Johnson became the first black man to win the heavyweight boxing championship, taking the title in 1908. Later, in 1937, Joe Louis, the "Brown Bomber" from Detroit, Michigan, won the title and held it for 12 years. Also in sports, the Native American athlete Jim Thorpe starred in college football and at the 1912 Olympics. Another Olympic champion was the black athlete Jesse Owens, who gained acclaim in Berlin at the 1936 Olympics, which were staged by

During the first half of the 20th century, black Americans established themselves in many fields. The boxer Joe Louis was one of the great heavyweight champions, holding the title for twelve years.

Nazi dictator Adolf Hitler in an effort, ironically, to demonstrate the supremacy of the Aryan race.

Noted black authors of the era included Langston Hughes, Richard Wright, W.E.B. DuBois, Jessie Fauset, and Zora Neale Hurston. In scientific fields, George Washington Carver—working at Tuskegee—developed new products from peanuts and sweet potatoes, while the physician Charles Drew discovered a way to preserve blood for transfusions.

Certainly not to be overlooked are the thousands of blacks and other minority members who served in both world wars—even though the U.S. military was as segregated as any other institution. In World War I, the 369th Infantry, an all-black regiment, saw combat in France. Its members served with a white French battalion, and, by the end of the war, 171 men of the 369th Infantry had been awarded the Croix de Guerre, France's highest military medal.

And yet, even as black soldiers fought to defend freedom in the trenches thousands of miles from America, they still found the shadow of Jim Crow hovering over them. In a directive to French military leaders, General John Pershing, commander of the American Expeditionary Force, wrote: "We must prevent the rise of any pronounced degree of intimacy between French officers and black officers. . . . We must not eat with them, shake hands with them, seek to talk to them and meet with them outside the requirements of military service. . . . White Americans become very incensed at any particular expression of intimacy between white women and black men."

Black soldiers fought bravely in World War II as well; again, though, the American armed forces were segregated. Perhaps no unit of black Americans trained harder or fought with more resolve than the Tuskegee Airmen, a group of pilots who trained at Tuskegee Army Air Field in Alabama and went on to fight in the 99th Fighter Squadron and 332nd Fighter Group. The Tuskegee Airmen flew combat missions in North Africa and Europe. Their accomplishments included sinking a German warship, destroying dozens of German troop and supply trains, shooting down one of the first German jets to fly in the war, and protecting American bombers on more than two hundred missions.

Members of the 369th Colored Infantry arrive in New York City after the end of World War I. This African-American regiment was highly decorated by the French government for its service in the trenches of western Europe.

CROSSING NEW BOUNDARIES

By the end of World War II, however, the cry for civil rights in the United States was too loud to ignore. In the South, many politicians, including Strom Thurmond, continued to preach segregation. However, during the 1948 election President Harry Truman made civil rights a major plank of the Democratic Party's platform. He pledged to end racial discrimination at the polls—literacy tests had prevented many black Americans from casting ballots. He also promised the authority of the U.S. government in the fight against racial discrimination. Truman ordered the armed forces desegregated—soldiers of all colors would now fight side by side—and he also ordered that blacks and other minorities be given equal opportunity to obtain jobs in the federal government.

During the 1948 presidential campaign, Harry S. Truman proposed various civil-rights reforms, including the creation of governmental departments that would protect voting rights and fair employment practices for minorities. He also issued Executive Order 9981 that year, which mandated integration of the U.S. military.

Americans greeted Truman's policies with a measure of support, although they were clearly wary of desegregation and its consequences. In 1948, a Gallup poll found that 49 percent of Americans thought railroad cars should be desegregated, while 43 percent believed blacks and whites should not have to ride in the same cars. In a separate Gallup poll in 1948, just 13 percent of respondents supported the president's plan to desegregate the military; 32 percent of the respondents believed military segregation should continue.

Black Americans also started to use the courts to achieve their goals. By the early 1950s, cases challenging the Supreme Court's 1896 *Plessy v. Ferguson* ruling had been filed in South Carolina, Virginia, Delaware, and Kansas. The Kansas case, filed by a black clergyman named Oliver Brown on behalf of his eight-year-old daughter Linda, ultimately became the case that would overturn the separate-but-equal doctrine in society and clear the way for desegregation of American schools.

Brown v. Board of Education of Topeka, Kansas was filed in 1951, and eventually heard by the U.S. Supreme Court. Lawyers for the plaintiffs argued that the education Linda Brown was receiving at an all-black, segregated school was far inferior to the education white students in Topeka received at their schools. Brown's lawyers, who included Thurgood Marshall, a future Supreme Court justice, received help from the U.S. government in making their case. President Dwight D. Eisenhower assigned Attorney General Herbert Brownell to argue against racial discrimination before the court.

A portrait of the young black students for whom the famous *Brown v. Board of Education* case was brought, along with their parents. Pictured are (front, left to right) Vicki Henderson, Donald Henderson, Linda Brown, James Emanuel, Nancy Todd, Katherine Carper; (back) Zelma Henderson, Oliver Brown, Sadie Emanuel, Lucinda Todd, and Lena Carper.

The Supreme Court handed down its decision in May 1954, ruling unanimously that separate-but-equal treatment was unconstitutional. U.S. Chief Justice Earl Warren wrote that "in the field of public education the doctrine of 'separate but equal' has no place" because schools are "inherently unequal." Warren stated that the separate-but-equal doctrine violates the Fourteenth Amendment to the U.S. Constitution, which guarantees equal rights to all citizens. He wrote:

> We must consider public education in the light of its full development and its present place in American life throughout the Nation. . . .
>
> Today, education is perhaps the most important function of state and local governments. Compulsory school attendance laws and the great expenditures for education both demonstrate our recognition of the importance of education to our democratic society. . . . It is the very foundation of good citizenship. Today it is a principal instrument in awakening the child to cultural values, in preparing him for later professional training, and in helping him to adjust normally to his environment. . . .
>
> To separate [children] from others of similar age and qualifications solely because of their race generates a feeling of inferiority as to their status in the community that may affect their hearts and minds in a way unlikely ever to be undone. . . . The effect of this separation on their educational opportunities was well stated by a finding in the Kansas case . . . :
>
>> Segregation of white and colored children in public schools has a detrimental effect upon the colored children. The impact is greater when it has the sanction of law, for the policy of separating the races is usually interpreted as denoting the inferiority of the negro group. A sense of inferiority affects the motivation of a child to learn. Segregation with the sanction of law, therefore, has a tendency to [retard] the educational and mental development of negro children and to deprive them of some of the benefits they would receive in a racial[ly] integrated school system.

A subsequent ruling by the court ordered public schools desegregated "with all deliberate speed." Again, Americans reacted with a measure of support to the Supreme Court's ruling—but the support was not overwhelming. A Gallup poll taken shortly after the *Brown v. Board of Education* decision found that just 22 percent of respondents believed schools should be desegregated immediately, as the Supreme Court had ruled. In contrast, 33 percent of respondents believed school desegregation should take place over a period of years, and 40 percent believed schools should remain segregated.

Thurgood Marshall, the attorney for the plaintiffs in *Brown v. Board of Education*, later became the first African American appointed to the U.S. Supreme Court.

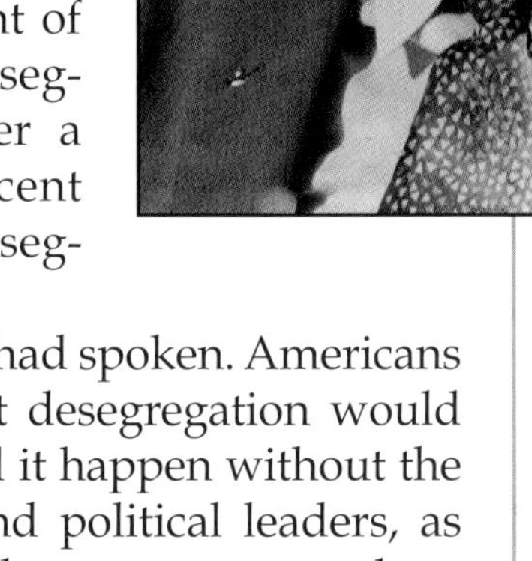

But the nation's highest court had spoken. Americans soon would learn, however, that desegregation would not happen overnight, nor would it happen without the efforts of civil rights activists and political leaders, as well as the grim resolve of some brave young people to cross boundaries that never had been crossed before.

3 "FREE AT LAST!"

Rosa Parks (front row, center) and other members of the black community in Montgomery, Alabama, listen as the Reverend Martin Luther King Jr. discusses the progress of the bus boycott, 1957. Parks's refusal to give up her seat on a crowded bus was a key moment in the civil rights movement.

The woman who emerged as one of the most important figures in the civil rights movement was not a fiery orator who inspired boldness with her words. Nor was she a rabble-rouser; she had been active in civil rights organizations, but everyone who knew Rosa Parks thought of her as more of a follower than a leader. And yet, on December 1, 1955, an act of courage by Parks sparked a defiant uprising among black people in the South, who took a bold stand against racial discrimination.

Parks worked as a seamstress in a Montgomery, Alabama, department store. On the evening of December 1, after finishing work she walked to a nearby corner to catch a bus for a ride home. Parks had been on her feet all day; she was looking forward to resting during the ride. When a bus arrived, she saw that it was crowded and that she would never get a seat, so she decided to wait for the next bus.

The operation of public buses in Montgomery was a prime example of Jim Crow in its purest form. Although the *Brown v. Board of Education* ruling the previous year had struck down the concept of "separate-but-equal" in schools, the Supreme Court's decision did not address other places where segregation existed—buses, movie theaters, restaurants, public restrooms, and trains, for example. As a result, these places were still legally segregated. On public buses throughout the South, whites were entitled to sit up front, while blacks were made to sit in the rear. In Montgomery, the whites were entitled to the first ten rows of seats. If a bus became crowded and the first ten rows were filled, blacks sitting behind them were expected to give up their seats and move further into the back of the bus. What's more, blacks were not allowed to enter the bus through the front door. They were made to pay in the front of the bus, then had to go back outside and re-enter by the rear door to take their seats. Such discrimination was not limited to Montgomery; similar restrictions on blacks were in place throughout the South.

When the next bus arrived, Rosa Parks found a seat in the black section and settled in for the ride home. Soon, the bus filled with passengers. When, finally, white passengers boarded the bus and were unable to find seats in the white section, the bus driver stopped the vehicle and shouted to the four black passengers at the front of the black section to give up their seats. Three of the passengers, all young black men, quietly rose and moved to the rear, but Rosa Parks, the fourth passenger, refused.

The driver stopped the vehicle and strode toward the back of the bus. He ordered Parks to give her seat to a white man, but Parks said she would not. When the driver threatened to have her arrested for violating Montgomery's racial segregation law, Parks told him to go ahead. When the police arrived, Parks again refused to give up her seat. She was arrested and jailed briefly, but soon bailed out by friends and black leaders who learned of the incident and rushed to post her bond.

News of Rosa Parks's arrest swept through the Montgomery black community. Soon, black leaders in the town called a meeting to discuss what their response should be. They decided to call for a boycott of the Montgomery public bus system by all black riders and to challenge Parks' arrest in the courts.

For the city's bus companies, the boycott pushed them to the verge of bankruptcy; black riders made up some two-thirds of the bus system's customers, and the companies could not afford to lose their business. The black riders who boycotted suffered as well; most of

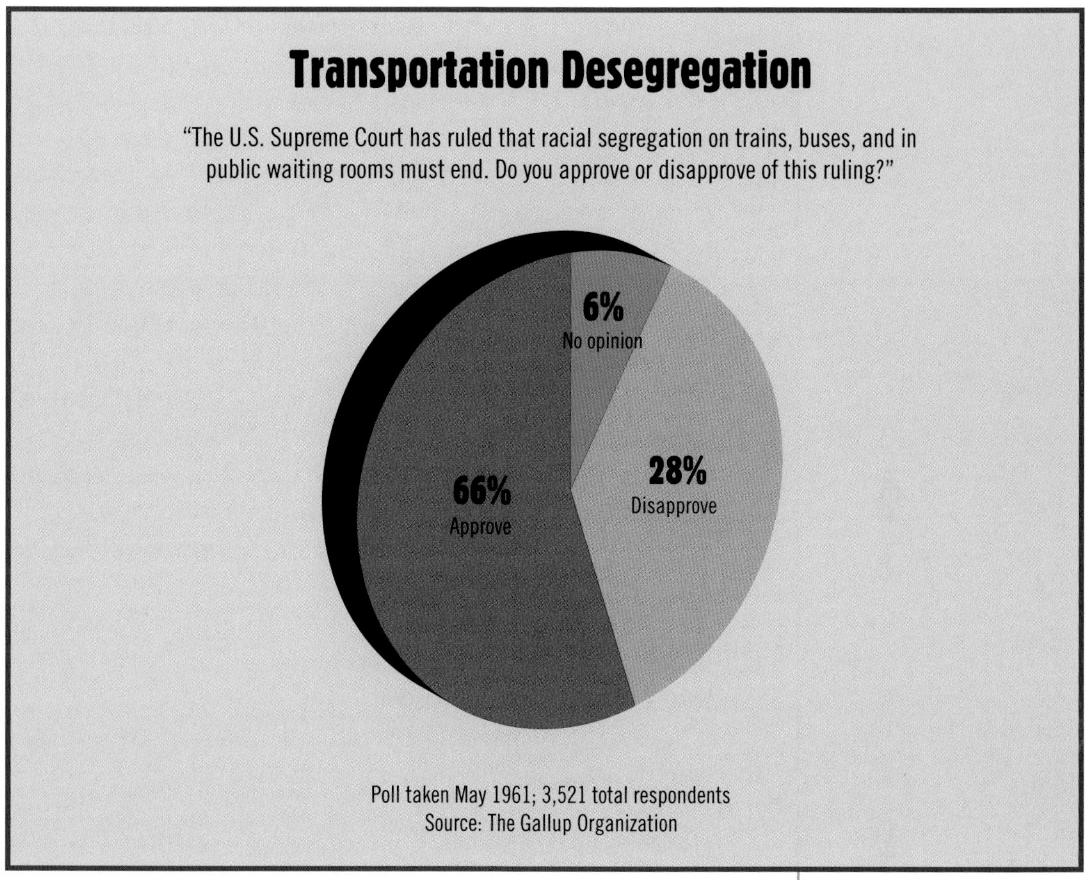

them were poor laborers who had no way to get to work other than by bus. Car pools organized by affluent blacks helped somewhat, but for most of the blacks of Montgomery, the year-long boycott was difficult to endure. Still, most of them stayed off the buses.

The boycott ended in December 1956. The bus companies, on the verge of economic collapse from losing so many customers, agreed to eliminate all segregation rules. Blacks could enter the bus in the front and sit anywhere they chose. Meanwhile, the Supreme Court ruled in late 1956 that the desegregation order applied to schools in *Brown v. Board of Education* applied to other public institutions as well. In 1961, a Gallup poll found that 66 percent of respondents agreed with the Supreme

Court's decision to end discrimination on public trains and buses and in waiting rooms.

Although Parks's act of defiance sparked the Montgomery bus boycott, the year-long protest was planned and organized by a group of black leaders who called themselves the Montgomery Improvement Association (MIA). Emerging as its leader was a young minister, Martin Luther King Jr., who headed a Baptist congregation in Montgomery. He was a visible and charismatic leader of the boycott and would go on to become the most important leader of the entire civil rights movement that exploded across the South.

On December 21, 1956, Martin Luther King Jr. took his first ride on a desegregated bus in Montgomery. He entered the bus through the front door and dropped his fare into the coin box.

The white driver said, "I believe you are Reverend King."

"Yes, I am," King responded.

"We are proud to have you with us this morning," the driver said.

THE LITTLE ROCK NINE

Soon after the Supreme Court handed down the *Brown v. Board of Education* decision, U.S. Attorney General Herbert Brownell met with the attorneys general of the southern states to discuss how they planned to implement school desegregation. He was hardly greeted with enthusiasm. None of the attorneys general, most of whom harbored political ambitions, wished to be first to implement desegregation and risk the wrath of pro-segregation white voters in their home states. And so desegregation proceeded slowly and sporadically—hardly the pace of "deliberate speed" that the Supreme Court had ordered.

In Little Rock, Arkansas, local school officials decided to admit nine black students to Little Rock Central High School for the school year that began in September

1957. Administrators spent months interviewing candidates, seeking top black students whom they believed could handle the workload but also warning them that they would face prejudice of the worst kind: racist taunts and perhaps beatings by white students. By the end of the summer, nine brave black students stepped forward and prepared to start school at Little Rock Central on September 3.

Arkansas Governor Orval Faubus found himself under intense pressure from whites to keep the "Little Rock Nine" out of a white high school. He was facing reelection himself and knew that he would be voted out of office if the nine black students were enrolled in the high school. A few days before school was scheduled to begin, Faubus announced that he feared rioting if the black students were permitted to enroll. He summoned the Arkansas National Guard on the pretext of maintaining order in Little Rock, but his real aim was to use the troops to block the Little Rock Nine's admission to the school.

When the first day of school arrived, the nine students approached the high school accompanied by civil rights activists and a Little Rock police car. They found members of the Arkansas National Guard surrounding the high school. Behind the soldiers stood an angry mob of whites. People in the crowd shouted racial slurs at the students and told them to go home. The students held their ground, though, until a National Guard captain stepped forward and told them that under the orders of Governor Faubus, they would not be permitted to enter the school.

Within a few weeks, the federal government ordered the guardsmen to leave the school. On September 23, 1957, the Little Rock Nine, escorted by policemen, made it into the school. However, the large crowd grew angry, and the students were subsequently removed from the school to avoid a tragic incident of violence. "The local police were not able to hold back the mob," recalled

Daisy Bates, an African-American activist in Arkansas, coordinated the integration of Little Rock's Central High School in 1957–58. She is standing here with the "Little Rock Nine": (front, left to right) Thelma Mothershed, Minnie Jean Brown, Elizabeth Eckford, Gloria Ray, (back) Jefferson Thomas, Melba Pattillo, Terrance Roberts, Carlotta Walls, Bates, and Ernest Green.

Elizabeth Eckford, one of the Little Rock Nine, in an interview with the Gallup Organization. "By that time, the mob had grown to 1,000 people and they were about to go into the school. Police took us out for our own protection."

Faubus won the first round, but the confrontation at the school was captured by television news cameras and seen by viewers around the country. During the late 1950s, television news was just starting to make an impact on American society. The three television networks had just recently launched evening news shows, and they all sent correspondents to Little Rock to cover the confrontation. The cameras captured the angry taunts of the mob as well as the armed soldiers turning away the nine students. The cameras also caught the action away from the school, as the rioters targeted innocent blacks. Some journalists were even physically assaulted by angry whites.

"One of the things that was significant about '57," Eckford said, "was that that was the first time that the public saw events in the context in which they happened. They didn't have to be reinterpreted by television reporters."

Television did impact the public's perception of the troubles in Little Rock. According to a 1957 Gallup poll taken between September 19 and September 24, 49 percent of respondents believed Little Rock Central High School should be integrated immediately, while 25 percent thought the integration plan should be delayed a year. Eighteen percent of the respondents said the school should never be integrated.

On September 24, 1957, President Eisenhower sent 1,000 soldiers from the U.S. Army's 101st Airborne

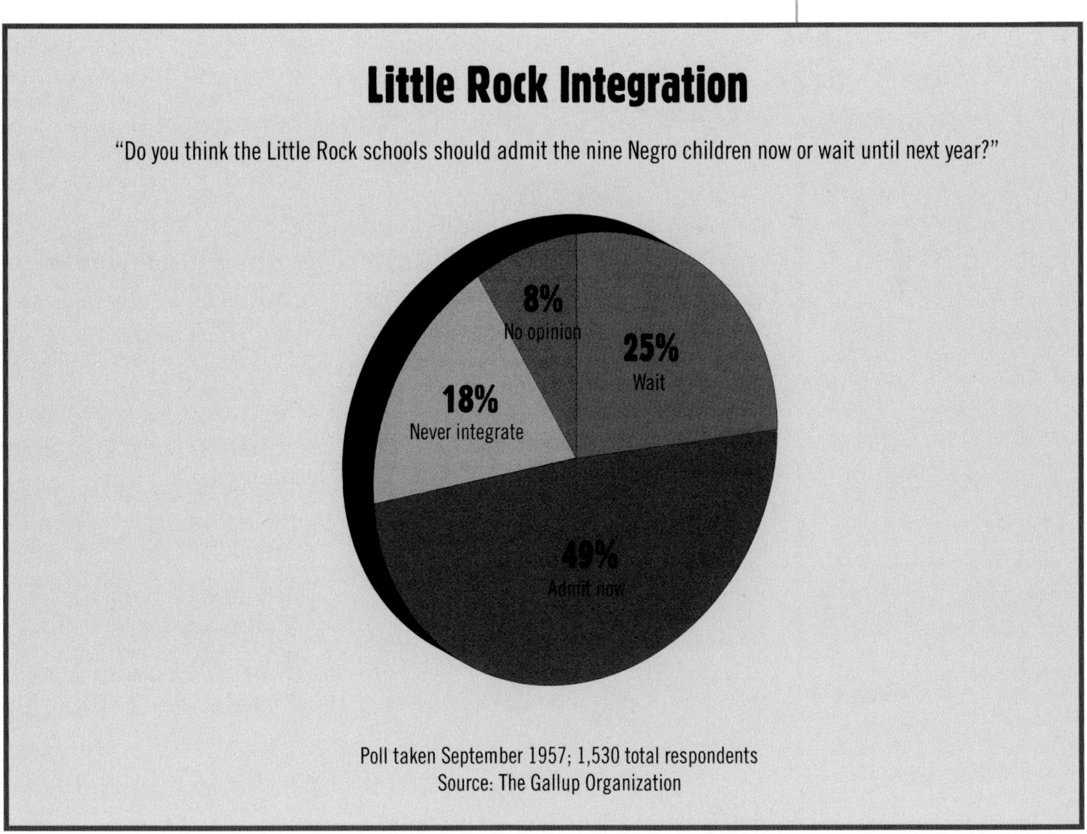

division to Little Rock. Additionally, he took command of the Arkansas National Guard away from Governor Faubus. The 101st Airborne arrived at the school and replaced the guardsmen. For the first time since the Civil War, federal troops were sent into a southern city. As for the nine black students, soldiers escorted them into the high school and also escorted them home at the end of the day.

Despite the victory, it would not be a pleasant year for the Little Rock Nine. Even with the protection of the 101st Airborne, the students still endured racist taunts, bullying, and physical abuse from white students. One of the students dropped out and returned to her segregated black high school. Eckford recalled that faculty members often looked the other way when trouble occurred. "If a teacher didn't see it, they didn't have to respond to it," she said. "I learned later, secondhand, that the principal had even said he wished the students would run us off the next year."

Actually, Eckford and the others would not return to Little Rock Central in 1958–59 but not because of the behaviors of fellow students. What kept them out once again was Faubus. Rather than continue the integration plan, Faubus closed all the high schools in the city for a year. The schools reopened in the fall of 1959, but it would take until 1972 for all grades in the Little Rock public school system to finally be integrated. As for Orval Faubus, Arkansas whites regarded him as a hero; they reelected him governor in 1958, and he remained in office until retiring at the end of 1966.

"I HAVE A DREAM"

Integrating other institutions of society proved more successful. By the late 1950s, for example, most major league baseball teams employed black players. Still, integration of baseball had had a rough start—the first black player, Jackie Robinson of the Brooklyn Dodgers, endured bitter racism during his rookie year of 1947.

Regardless, he turned in a stellar performance, earning Rookie of the Year honors and helping his team win the National League pennant.

By the late 1950s and early 1960s, there were black stars in other sports as well—Bill Russell and Wilt Chamberlain in basketball, Jim Brown and Ernie Davis in football, Sonny Liston and Cassius Clay in boxing. Popular music was also integrated, at least in terms of its consumers; parents may have feared integration in schools and bus terminals, but their white teenagers bought records by black artists such as Chuck Berry, Little Richard, Sam Cooke, and Fats Domino.

By the 1960s, African Americans like basketball player Wilt Chamberlain and singer Sam Cooke were popular among both white and black audiences.

Young people seemed far more willing to accept, and work for, integration than their parents. For decades, white-dominated state legislatures in the South had been able to bar many blacks from the polls, using literacy tests and other unconstitutional methods to discourage blacks from voting. During the 1960 presidential election, however, young college students from the northern states joined the ranks of the "freedom riders," spreading throughout the South by the busload to conduct voter registration drives in black communities and encourage blacks to vote.

In the early 1960s, other protests against segregation continued. In Greensboro, North Carolina, four black students sat down at a lunch counter at a Woolworth's and refused to leave until they were served, sparking similar "sit-in" demonstrations at dozens of other segregated restaurants. In Mississippi, 5,000 soldiers arrived at the University of Mississippi, sent by

Martin Luther King Jr. (1929–1968) was one of the most important leaders of the Civil Rights movement. In 1964 he received the Nobel Peace Prize for his efforts to fight racial prejudice using non-violent tactics.

President John F. Kennedy so that James Meredith, a black student, could enroll. In Birmingham, Alabama, television cameras caught police under the command of Sheriff Eugene "Bull" Connor turning fire hoses and police dogs on black protesters. Those televised images had a tremendous impact on public opinion. In June 1963, 82 percent of respondents to a Gallup poll said they believed the day would soon arrive when whites and blacks in the South would be welcome at the same schools, restaurants, and other American institutions.

That day would come, but not before blood was spilled. In 1963, Medgar Evers, an official of the Mississippi branch of the National Association for the Advancement of Colored People (NAACP), was murdered outside his home by a white segregationist. That same year, four black teenage girls lost their lives when a bomb exploded in their church in Birmingham, Alabama. A year later, three civil rights workers—Michael Schwerner, Andrew Goodman, and James Chaney—who were helping blacks register to vote, were murdered near the small town of Philadelphia, Mississippi.

But every time a life was lost or a protester was attacked by police, those in the civil rights movement seemed to have a hardening of resolve to win integration. By the early 1960s, Reverend Martin Luther King Jr. was a national leader of the movement. On August 28, 1963, King stood on the steps of the Lincoln Memorial and addressed a crowd of some 250,000 people gathered on the mall in Washington. In his speech, King eloquently set the goal for the civil rights movement.

Minorities would accept nothing less than equality in all aspects of American society, and all of society would benefit:

> I have a dream that one day this nation will rise up and live out the true meaning of its creed: "We hold these truths to be self-evident: that all men are created equal." I have a dream that one day on the red hills of Georgia the sons of former slaves and the sons of former slave owners will be able to sit down together at a table of brotherhood. I have a dream that one day even the state of Mississippi, a desert state, sweltering with the heat of injustice and oppression, will be transformed into an oasis of freedom and justice. I have a dream that my four children will one day live in a nation where they will not be judged by the color of their skin but by the content of their character. I have a dream today. . . .
>
> When we let freedom ring, when we let it ring from every village and every hamlet, from every state and every city, we will be able to speed up that day when all of God's children, black men and white men, Jews and Gentiles, Protestants and Catholics, will be able to join hands and sing in the words of the old Negro spiritual, "Free at last! Free at last! Thank God Almighty, we are free at last!"

"BECAUSE IT IS RIGHT"

In 1964, Congress responded by passing the Civil Rights Act. The law prohibited the exclusion of blacks and other minority members from hotels, theaters, restaurants, and all other public places. The act also empowered the U.S. Justice Department to bring lawsuits against school districts that refused to desegregate, banned the use of federal tax dollars for any activity that excluded minorities, and outlawed discrimination in the workplace and in union membership. The act had been proposed the year before by President Kennedy following a confrontation with segregationist Governor George Wallace, who refused to admit two black students to the University of Alabama. Wallace himself blocked the doorway of the

President Lyndon B. Johnson speaks to the nation before signing the Civil Rights Act, July 1964.

registration building until Kennedy federalized the Alabama National Guard, which ordered Wallace to move. Kennedy called for adoption of the Civil Rights Act "not merely for reasons of economic efficiency, world diplomacy and domestic tranquility—but above all because it is right." Kennedy was assassinated in November 1963, but the following year President Lyndon B. Johnson signed the bill into law.

In later years, Johnson promoted legislation for what he called the "Great Society." The legislation created a series of anti-poverty programs designed to help poor people, mostly blacks and Hispanics living in the inner cities. Johnson's Great Society programs were intended to help lift poor people out of poverty. The programs provided taxpayer-funded food, day care, education, and cash support to families who were living below the poverty line.

Still, many problems remained, and some blacks became angrier and more emboldened to act. Riots erupted in Watts, a poor black neighborhood in Los

Angeles, as well as in northern cities like Philadelphia, Newark, Detroit, and the Harlem section of New York. The era saw the emergence of militant black leaders such as Stokely Carmichael, as well as Bobby Seale and Huey P. Newton, founders of the Black Panther Party. Unlike King, an admirer of the nonviolent Mahatma Ghandi and a firm advocate of nonviolence himself, these black leaders suggested that violence should be employed to achieve equality. In July 1967, a Gallup poll asked Americans whether they feared "any serious racial trouble in this [their own] community in the next six months." Thirteen percent of the respondents answered that they did. Typical comments included:

> "There is tension between Negroes and law enforcement officials here."
>
> "Negroes are demanding too much."

Members of the Black Panther Party demonstrate outside a New York courthouse, 1969. The pace of racial change remained slow through the 1960s, and some frustrated African Americans rejected the nonviolent approach of Martin Luther King, advocating violence as a way to force society to change.

"Not enough is being done to prevent violence."

"Bad living conditions."

"Lack of jobs available to minority groups."

"The Negro has been held down too long."

"News media gives the impression that Negroes will use violence."

LA CAUSA

During this era, Hispanics also were making strides toward winning equality. They, too, had to fight hard for it. In the western states, many Hispanics found jobs as farm laborers, picking lettuce, grapes, and other crops on sprawling farms. Although most were hard workers, they were often treated unjustly. For such laborers, the work day lasted from dawn until sundown. The work was exhausting and the pay was low.

Many of the growers made use of *braceros*—Mexican citizens who received permission from the U.S. government to work on American farms. The bracero system had started during World War II because of the labor shortage created by the military draft. When the war ended, many politically influential growers persuaded Congress to keep the bracero system intact, claiming that labor shortages still existed. In reality, though, the growers preferred the bracero system because they could pay the Mexicans less than what American farm workers demanded.

In 1954, Cesar Chavez, a social worker and Hispanic community activist, started leading protests against the bracero system. Chavez had been born on an Arizona farm, but his family lost their land during the Great Depression and the Chavezes were forced to work as low-paid farm laborers. When Chavez returned from World War II, he dedicated himself to improving the plight of Hispanic farm workers. Working in California, Chavez organized picket lines at bracero camps and led demonstrations outside farms that abused the bracero system. Because of pressure from Chavez and other Hispanic leaders, Congress ultimately outlawed the use of bracero labor in 1964.

By the mid-1960s, Chavez was leading an effort to organize farm laborers into a new union, the United Farm Workers (UFW). For years, Chavez and other organizers traveled throughout California and the other western states to sign up laborers to join the union. In 1965, the union's membership consisted of a mere 1,700 dues-paying members; nevertheless, Chavez believed the UFW could bargain for better wages. The growers disagreed. The next five years would prove to be a contentious time in the farm labor movement. Strikes were called, and violence erupted on the picket lines as the growers dispatched thugs to disrupt the protests.

On March 17, 1966, Chavez led a 300-mile march from the California city of Delano to the state capital of Sacramento to dramatize the plight of the farm workers, labeling the march the *Perigrinacion,* or "Pilgrimage." Chavez and dozens of marchers stopped in migrant camps and Hispanic communities along the way for rallies. Arriving in Sacramento on April 10, Chavez spoke to the crowd and issued a warning to the growers: "You cannot close your eyes and your ears to us any longer. You cannot pretend that we do not exist. You cannot plead ignorance to our problems because we are here and we embody our needs for you. And we are not alone."

In 1968, Chavez called for a national boycott on grapes. Union leaders fanned out across thirty cities in the United States and Canada to publicize the boycott, handing out leaflets in supermarket parking lots, speaking to church groups, and leading rallies on college campuses. In Boston, farm workers staged a "Boston Grape Party." They led a march through city streets, ending at Boston Harbor, where several bushels of California

Hispanic labor activist Cesar Chavez (center), surrounded by grape pickers, walks through a field in Delano, California. Chavez struggled to establish the United Farm Workers in order to help workers, many of whom were minorities, gain better wages and working conditions.

grapes were dumped into the water. In New York, a city transit union helped the Farm Workers by printing and distributing a million leaflets announcing the boycott. Other unions also joined the movement, and eventually, some 50 million leaflets admonishing people to boycott grapes were distributed in North America. Chavez called the boycott *La Causa,* meaning "the cause."

By 1968, the California grape growers reported sales had fallen by some 20 percent. Also, the reduced demand for table grapes caused their prices to drop by about 15 percent during the first year of the strike. A year later, the growers reported that the boycott had cost them $25 million.

In 1970, the growers caved in and agreed to bargain with the United Farm Workers. The union won its workers a wage of $1.80 an hour—eighty cents more an hour than they had been earning. The growers also agreed to establish a medical insurance plan for the laborers and to monitor the farms' use of pesticides, which the union believed was responsible for many of the workers' health problems. At the end of the long and grueling strike and boycott, Chavez said, "The strikers and the people involved in this struggle sacrificed a lot, sacrificed all of their worldly possessions. Ninety-five percent of the strikers lost their homes and their cars. But I think in losing those worldly possessions they found themselves."

TWO SOCIETIES

During the 1960s, no civil rights leader preached nonviolence as a course of action more than Rev. Martin Luther King Jr. Yet on April 4, 1968, King was assassinated as he emerged onto the balcony of a motel in Memphis, Tennessee, where he had gone to give his support to striking black garbage collectors. His killer was James Earl Ray, a racist white drifter. For King's funeral, more than 100,000 mourners lined the streets of Atlanta, Georgia, while an estimated audience of 120 million people watched the news coverage of the

JESSE JACKSON'S CAMPAIGNS FOR THE PRESIDENCY

One of the civil rights workers who had accompanied Martin Luther King Jr. to Memphis in 1968 was Jesse Jackson, a young minister from Chicago. Following King's assassination, Jackson went on to found People United to Save Humanity (PUSH) and the Rainbow Coalition, two groups that would make Jackson an influential voice in the civil rights movement.

By 1984, Jackson was perhaps the most visible and familiar civil rights leader in the United States. That year, he launched the first of his two candidacies for the Democratic nomination for president.

Jackson was not the first African American to run for president. Back in 1972, Shirley Chisholm, a black congresswoman from New York City, became the first black candidate to be regarded as a serious contender for a major party's presidential nomination. She was never able to break into her party's top tier of candidates, however. Campaigning in the spring of 1972, Chisholm won only about 7 percent of the vote during the Democratic primaries.

In 1984, Jackson proved to be a much more formidable contender. He carried on a relentless campaign that won widespread support among minority voters, although whites were less willing to back him. Specifically, many whites were disturbed by the support given to Jackson by Louis Farrakhan, leader of the Nation of Islam, a Black Muslim faction that called for black separatism. Jewish voters were also troubled by Jackson; in 1979, the candidate had embraced Palestinian leader Yasir Arafat, whose Palestine Liberation Organization opposed Israel's right to exist and supported terrorism. What's more, in remarks to reporters that Jackson thought were off the record, he referred to New York City, which has a large Jewish population, with an anti-Semitic slur. Jackson apologized for the remark, but his campaign was in trouble. A Gallup poll taken in April 1984 found that 33 percent of respondents believed his remarks had created bad feelings between blacks and Jews. Also, 61 percent of

funeral on television. King was buried in the South View Cemetery in Atlanta. On his crypt were the words he had quoted in his "I Have a Dream" speech: "Free at Last, Free at Last, Thank God Almighty I'm Free at Last."

King's work would live on. Over the next four decades, blacks and other minority members would make tremendous strides in winning equality. Congress passed additional civil rights legislation, banning discrimination in housing and making it respondents opposed Jackson's support for Yasir Arafat and the PLO. Still, Jackson received 3.5 million votes and won 5 primaries, all in the South. He finished a surprising third behind former vice president Walter Mondale and Senator Gary Hart.

Four years later, in April 1988, a Gallup poll found that just 25 percent of respondents still felt Jackson was responsible for bad feelings between blacks and Jews. Although initially, few people in the media thought Jackson had a chance to win the nomination, he increased his vote total to 6.9 million, and won primaries in Alabama, Georgia, Louisiana, Mississippi, Virginia, and Washington, D.C. In many other states, Jackson finished a strong second behind the eventual nominee, Michael Dukakis, the governor of Massachusetts.

Jackson's support was limited mostly to minority voters, but he nevertheless received their overwhelming support during the primaries. A Gallup poll of minorities in April 1988 found 83 percent of black voters favoring Jackson's election over Vice President George H.W. Bush, who was the presumptive Republican nominee.

A Gallup analysis of Jackson's 1988 candidacy found that voters gave him high marks on social issues but believed he lacked the experience and expertise in foreign affairs and the economy that they would expect of a presidential candidate. Said the Gallup analysis: "Solid majorities of voters give Jackson high marks for his honesty and sincerity (72%), as a champion of social justice (60%), and as a strong and forceful leader (56%). However, pluralities doubt that he is capable of dealing with the complex issues that face a president, or that he could manage the federal government, deal effectively with foreign leaders, or improve respondents' economic conditions. Substantial numbers also question Jackson's ability, if elected, to represent all Americans, and they criticize his stands on the issues as too extreme."

easier for employees to sue their employers for discrimination. Civil rights laws also would be extended to ensure fair treatment of women and the handicapped. Additionally, the sacrifices made by the freedom riders in the early 1960s would pay dividends: blacks would exert their influence at the polls, using their majorities in southern cities to elect mayors and representatives to Congress. Hispanics, Asians, and other minorities would also benefit from the civil rights movement.

Soldiers stand guard in the streets of a black neighborhood in Washington, D.C.; rubble from destroyed buildings can be seen in the background, as can a fire truck attempting to extinguish a fire set by rioters in the aftermath of Martin Luther King's April 1968 assassination.

And yet, for Americans, the road toward equality would continue to be bumpy. In 1968, President Johnson appointed Governor Otto Kerner of Illinois to head the National Advisory Commission on Civil Disorders. Among the findings of the Kerner Commission was that America was moving toward "two societies, one black and one white—separate and unequal." When a Gallup poll asked Americans to respond to the findings of the commission, 36 percent of respondents agreed with them. Indeed, as events would unfold, there was reason to believe that the Kerner Commission's prediction might be on track.

During the 1980s, for example, a conservative political movement would grow in the United States; its leaders started scaling back the 1960s Great Society antipoverty programs, whose beneficiaries included tens of thousands of inner-city minority families.

At the same time, racism continued to exist, although to some degree this occurred below the surface.

4 THE RACIAL PROFILING DEBATE

A highway patrolman speaks to a driver he has pulled over at a traffic checkpoint. In recent years controversy has erupted over racial profiling, which occurs when motorists are stopped on suspicion of criminal activity for no reason other than their skin color or other racial characteristics.

In 1992 Robert Wilkins, a Harvard University-educated attorney, was driving three relatives on a Maryland highway when a state trooper signaled him to pull over to the side. Once Wilkins stopped, the trooper ordered him and his passengers to step out of the car and then the trooper searched the vehicle.

In an interview with a news reporter after the incident, Wilkins said, "When I pushed him as to why he thought we were suspicious, and why he thought he had a right to do this, he said, 'Well, we're having a problem with rental cars and drugs.' And that wasn't really a satisfactory response because, as I told him, I said, 'I know you are not stopping everyone in a rental car and searching them. And driving a rental car isn't any reason for you to think that somebody is suspicious and they might have drugs.'"

Wilkins suspected that the trooper stopped his car simply because he is African American. This is a practice known as "racial profiling," in which it is common for police officers to regard minorities as suspects in criminal activities simply on the basis of their race. Wilkins sued the Maryland State Police and won a settlement of $96,000. What's more, the settlement also required state police in Maryland to keep records of the race and gender of drivers that they stop.

People have long suspected that racial profiling is widespread in the United States. In 1998, the practice erupted into a national scandal when two New Jersey state policemen shot and wounded three unarmed black and Hispanic youths who were traveling in a van the police had stopped. The attorney for the victims, Johnnie

Cochran, alleged that there was nothing about the van that would have prompted the state troopers to pull it over and that if it had been driven by a white man it would not have been stopped. As a result, the victims won a $12 million settlement from the state, after which Cochran said, "By virtue of the actions of these young men and our representation of them, we have now had [New Jersey] acknowledge racial profiling existing for a substantial period of time."

In 2001, the U.S. Justice Department studied the issue and concluded that in 1999, 12 percent of all licensed drivers pulled over by police that year were black. That statistic doesn't sound as though blacks are singled out for traffic stops, but the Justice Department also found that of the blacks and Hispanics who were pulled over, some 11 percent were searched. The study found that just 5 percent of white drivers were searched. In 90 percent of all cases, the Justice Department said, no evidence of criminal wrongdoing was uncovered.

NATIONAL SCANDAL

Although it took until the late 1990s for racial profiling to surface as a national scandal, the practice actually has a long and unpleasant history in the United States. One infamous case in which all members of a racial group were suspected of activity solely on the basis of their race occurred during World War II, when more than 110,000 Japanese Americans were regarded as security risks and forced to live in internment camps.

The internment of Japanese Americans—most of whom had no connection to or sympathy with Japan—was challenged in the courts by a Japanese American named Fred Korematsu. The U.S. Supreme Court heard the case and in December 1944 ruled that the deprivation of Korematsu's freedom did not violate the due process or equal justice provisions of the U.S. Constitution. Instead, the court said that during times

Members of a Japanese-American family, wearing identification tags, wait for the bus that will take them from their home in Hayward, California, to an internment camp, May 1942.

of national crises, such as war, the government has a responsibility to protect its citizens. Korematsu's internment, said the Supreme Court, had a "definite and close relationship to the prevention of espionage and sabotage."

And yet, following the attack on Pearl Harbor, the nation found itself at war not only with Japan but with Germany and Italy as well. German Americans and Italian Americans, however, were not rounded up and sent to camps for the duration of the war.

In the decades after World War II ended, the U.S. government officially recognized that its policy had negatively affected the lives of numerous Japanese-American families. The government officially apologized for the internment program, and offered compensation to many of those affected.

A LAW-ENFORCEMENT TOOL

As a tool for law enforcement, racial profiling may be regarded as an outgrowth of the widely accepted practice of "criminal profiling"—the use of psychologists, sociologists, and mental health experts to develop a profile of a type of person most likely to commit a certain type of crime. The Federal Bureau of Investigation pioneered this technique, developing the profile, which does have a racial element, of the typical serial killer: a white male loner. In a particular case of serial murder, then, unless police unearth evidence to the contrary—such as an eyewitness account—the FBI's work means that police start their search looking for suspects who fit the profile.

"Criminal profiling has come into increasing use over the last twenty years, not just as a way to solve particular crimes police know about but also as a way to predict who may be involved in as-yet-undiscovered crimes, especially drug offenses," says Toledo College of Law professor David A. Harris, author of *Profiles in Injustice*. "Criminal profiling is designed to help police spot criminals by developing sets of personal and behavioral characteristics associated with particular offenses. By comparing individuals they observe with profiles, officers should have a better basis for deciding which people to treat as suspects. Officers may see no direct evidence of crime, but they can rely on noncriminal but observable characteristics associated with crime to decide whether someone seems suspicious and therefore deserving of greater police scrutiny."

Sometimes those "observable characteristics" may include the choice of car. Minorities driving fancy or expensive vehicles are more likely to be stopped and searched by police. Robert Richards, a black Baltimore policeman, told a reporter, "I see a 16-year-old white boy in a [Mercedes] Benz, I think, 'Damn, that boy's daddy is rich.' I see a 16-year-old black, I think, 'That boy's slinging drugs."

DRUG MULES

During the 1980s and 1990s, it became clear to state police departments patrolling highways on the East Coast—particularly Interstate 95, which runs from Florida to Maine—that many people arrested for drug offenses were black or Hispanic. Florida has long been a major point of entry for illegal drugs smuggled into the country by Latin American drug gangs. So-called "mules"—people willing to carry drugs to the large Northeastern cities—are easily hired in the black and Hispanic ghettos of Miami and other Florida cities. A 2002 Drug Threat Assessment issued by the National Drug Intelligence Center warned, "Maryland's proximity to New York City and its strategic location on the Interstate 95 corridor between New York City and Miami make it an important node in drug supply routes on the East Coast. Drugs typically are transported into and through Maryland on Interstates 95 and 81, two major north-south highways on the East Coast." The Threat Assessment was quite clear about who distributes drugs in Maryland. It stated:

> Gangs distribute drugs, particularly heroin, cocaine and marijuana, at the retail level in Maryland. According to the Washington/Baltimore HIDTA [High Intensity Drug Trafficking Area Program], 60 percent of the gangs in Maryland are African American, 20 percent are Caucasian, and the remaining 20 percent are Asian, Hispanic, or Jamaican. . . . The Mid-Atlantic Gang Investigators Network reports that gangs involved in drug distribution have migrated from Florida and New York and have formed drug distribution networks in western Maryland.

Urban street gangs such as the Bloods, Crips, and Latin Kings, whose members are predominantly minorities, are heavily involved in the illegal drug trade and other criminal activities.

The Threat Assessment identified four ethnic gangs as responsible for much of the drug activity in Maryland: the black gangs known as the Bloods and the Crips; the Latin Kings, a Hispanic street gang that migrated east from Chicago; and Mara Salvatrucha, a street gang whose members emigrated from El Salvador. Said Clayton Searle, president of the International Narcotics Interdiction Association, "Those who purport to be shocked that ethnic groups are over-represented in the population arrested for certain criminal activities must have been in a prolonged coma. The fact is that ethnic groups control the majority of organized criminal activity in the United States. They also tend to hire as their underlings and couriers others of their same group. Why? Because these are the people they grew up with, feel comfortable around, and because it's human nature."

And so when police in Maryland and other East Coast regions started targeting black and Hispanic motorists for traffic stops, it was done in the belief that law-enforcement officials were more likely to find drugs in those cars than in cars driven by white people. Some studies have supported that theory. In 2001, University of Pennsylvania professors John Knowles, Nicola Persico, and Petra Todd performed a statistical analysis of traffic stops along Interstate 95 in Maryland and concluded that black drivers were more likely than white drivers to be drug couriers.

Knowles, Persico, and Todd studied traffic stops on Interstate 95 in Maryland from 1995 through 1999 and found that black drivers constituted 63 percent of the motorists who were stopped and searched by police, even though they accounted for just 18 percent of the motorists on the road. Whites accounted for 29 percent of the traffic stops, while Hispanics constituted 6 percent of the stops. The authors of the study said black and Hispanic drivers seemed to observe the traffic laws as carefully as white drivers—they didn't switch lanes without signaling and didn't exceed the speed limit to a greater degree than whites did, for example—and so there seemed to be no other reason they were being stopped than because of their race.

Knowles, Persico, and Todd said they examined the records of some fifteen hundred police searches and found a high proportion of blacks and Hispanics searched who were driving expensive luxury cars between the hours of midnight and six o'clock in the morning. After checking arrest records, the researchers concluded that Hispanics are twice as likely as whites to be carrying large quantities of drugs, and blacks are more than four times as likely as whites to be carrying large quantities of drugs. The authors wrote: "When we look at the probability of being found with drugs in large quantities, this probability tends to be higher for African-American drivers."

Similarly, Rutgers University professor Jackson Toby in a *Wall Street Journal* column, remarked, "If drug traffickers are disproportionately black or Hispanic, the police don't need to be racist to stop many minority motorists; they simply have to be efficient in targeting potential drug traffickers."

Maryland State Trooper Mike Lewis told a reporter that when he patrolled the rural Eastern Shore region of the state, most of the drug offenders he arrested were poor whites. In most cases, he said, the offenders were charged with carrying small quantities of drugs. When he started patrolling interstate highways, he began making bigger busts, but all of the drivers he arrested were minorities. "Ask me how many white people I've ever arrested for cocaine smuggling—ask me," he demanded of a *New York Times Magazine* reporter. "None! Zero! I debrief hundreds of black smugglers, and I ask them, 'Why don't you hire white guys to deliver your drugs?' They just laugh at me. 'We ain't gonna trust our drugs with white boys.' That's what they say."

Police argue that all races are profiled, not just blacks and Hispanics. For example, two black plainclothes detectives, Mark Robinson and Greg Jones, regularly patrol the Logan section of Philadelphia. It is a depressed, economically disadvantaged, drug-ridden, and largely black and Hispanic area of the city. Whenever the two black detectives spot young whites in a Logan neighborhood, they conclude that the whites are in the area for one reason and one reason only: to buy drugs. Jones spotted four young whites on a Logan street corner late one night. "No reason for them to be around here at this time of night, nope," Jones told a

Advocates of the importance of considering race to effective police work argue that it is not just minorities who are profiled. For example, whites who visit predominantly black or Hispanic neighborhoods may be stopped by police who suspect they are trying to purchase drugs.

reporter. "You're a cop. You know who's committing the crimes. It's your neighborhood. That's how it works."

RACIAL PROFILING WIDESPREAD

Still, many law enforcement officials and political leaders have acknowledged that police violate the constitutional rights of innocent blacks and other minority members if they single them out as suspects for no other reason than the color of their skin. "Profiling means a police officer using cumulative knowledge and training to identify certain indicators of possible criminal activity," said former New Jersey Governor Christine Todd Whitman in a statement at the height of the racial-profiling controversy in New Jersey during the late 1990s. "Race may be one of those factors, but it cannot stand alone. Racial profiling is when race is the only factor. There's no other probable cause."

Racial profiling doesn't occur just on highways. In 2004, the human rights group Amnesty International USA released a report titled *Threat and Humiliation: Racial Profiling, Domestic Security and Human Rights in the United States*. The report detailed dozens of cases of racial profiling in shopping malls, stores, and airports. Amnesty International USA cited this case, involving Sharon Simmons-Thomas, an African American woman from New York, as typical of how blacks fall under suspicion by store security guards:

> Last December . . . [Ms.] Simmons stopped in . . . [a major department store] to do a little quick shopping. When leaving the store, she was apprehended by two plainclothes security guards. "They wouldn't say who they were, but they accused me of shoplifting," she said. The guards refused to look at the receipts Simmons waved in their face. She was handcuffed, paraded in front of other customers, and then escorted to the store's detention cells, which are just atrocious. "I've never been so embarrassed in my life," she continued. In the detention cells were several other customers being held as suspect[ed] shoplifters, all of them people of color. "They ran a background

> check on me and discovered I didn't have a criminal record," she said. Three hours later, after being humiliated by a body search, threatened with physical force and attempts to coerce a false confession, she was freed but without her [purchases]."

PROFILING TO PREVENT TERRORISM

Following the September 11, 2001, terrorist attacks in which Arab highjackers took over airliners and flew them into the World Trade Center in New York and the Pentagon near Washington, D.C., federal authorities enacted security measures at airports in an effort to ensure people do not board airplanes while carrying weapons or explosives. Since then, according to Amnesty International USA, there have been many occasions when people of Arab, Persian and South Asian ethnicity have been singled out at airports and subjected to abusive searches.

The organization cited the case of Sandra Rama and her young son Omar, who live in Tulsa, Oklahoma. (Ironically, Sandra Rama serves on the Tulsa Police Community Race Relations Committee.) Rama and her son arrived at an airport, with Rama wearing the traditional Muslim head covering for women and her son carrying a model car he had built for a Boy Scout project. "Imagine how I felt when my eight-year-old son was pulled from the line because of his name and I could not go with him," she said. "Imagine how he felt when they started to take apart his Boy Scout pinewood derby car in the Boy Scout box. . . . It is now routine for my son, for Omar Rama, to get extra security checks at the airport. He knows it's going to happen, and he expects it. . . . But how do I tell my . . . son that it's okay? He is now ten. He is learning about civil liberties and civil rights. What meaning do they have for him?"

In a 2004 poll, the Gallup Organization found that 53 percent of respondents believed racial profiling of motorists on highways is widespread in the United

A man passes through a security checkpoint at Miami International Airport. In the wake of the September 11, 2001, terrorist attacks on the United States by Arab Muslim fanatics, U.S. airports intensified their procedures for screening passengers. However, this has prompted complaints of discrimination from both Arab Americans and Muslims.

States. The Gallup poll respondents agreed that racial profiling is not limited to highways. For instance, 49 percent of the respondents said they believe security guards in malls tend to keep an eye on blacks and Hispanics more often because they consider them to be likely shoplifters. Also, 43 percent of the respondents said they believe racial profiling is employed at security checkpoints at airports—clearly a reaction to the terrorist attacks of September 11.

Those numbers were compiled after interviews with whites as well as minorities. Not surprisingly, when the answers are categorized by ethnicity, it is clear that blacks and Hispanics feel much more strongly about the degree of racial profiling that exists in American society.

For example, 67 percent of blacks and 63 percent of Hispanics feel racial profiling is employed in traffic stops, whereas just 50 percent of white respondents believe this. As for airport checks, 54 percent of Hispanics, 48 percent of blacks, and 40 percent of

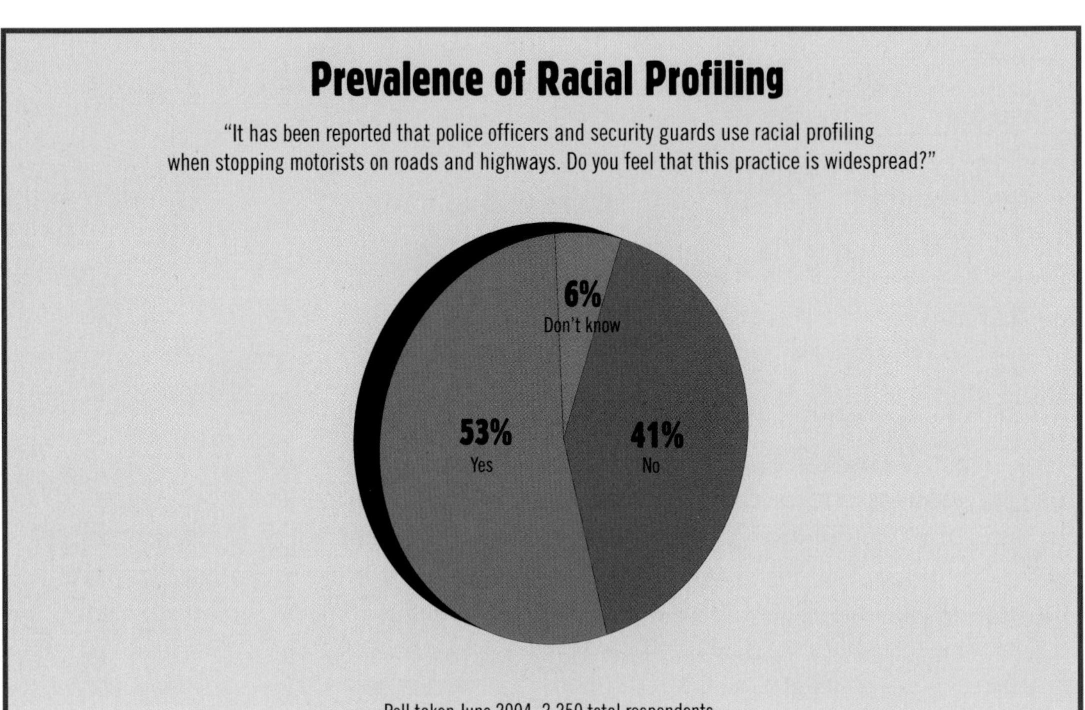

whites say guards employ racial profiling at airport security stations. Also, 65 percent of blacks, 56 percent of Hispanics, and 45 percent of whites feel racial profiling is widespread in shopping malls.

As to whether racial profiling is justified, according to the Gallup poll, 25 percent of respondents feel it is justified in shopping malls, 31 percent believe the practice is justified on the highways, and 45 percent of respondents favor employing racial profiling at airport security stations—again, probably a reaction to the 2001 terrorist attacks.

When the answers are categorized by ethnicity, the Gallup polls show no clear findings. On the highway, racial profiling is endorsed by 23 percent of black respondents, 30 percent of Hispanics, and 31 percent of whites. In the airports, racial profiling is much more accepted, with 32 percent of blacks, 40 percent of

Hispanics, and 46 percent of whites supporting its use to prevent airliner hijackings. The results are much more mixed when respondents are questioned about profiling in shopping malls, however. In this case, 19 percent of blacks but 38 percent of Hispanics favor racial profiling in malls to prevent shoplifting, while whites fall in between with 24 percent feeling it is justified.

UNDERMINING THE LEGITIMACY OF THE LAW

By 2005, twenty-three state legislatures had passed laws banning racial profiling by police and the U.S. Justice Department had adopted guidelines prohibiting the use of racial profiling by federal law enforcement agencies, such as the Federal Bureau of Investigation and the Drug Enforcement Administration.

Still, as the Gallup results indicate, racial profiling continues to be widespread. According to Amnesty International USA, from 2001 to 2004 some 32 million minority Americans have been questioned or searched by police simply because of their ethnicity. Amnesty International USA's report, *Threat and Humiliation*, said:

- ✓ Approximately 87 million Americans are at a high risk of being subjected to future racial profiling during their lifetime.
- ✓ Racial profiling directly affects Native Americans, Asian Americans, Hispanic Americans, African Americans, Arab Americans, Persian Americans, American Muslims, many immigrants and visitors, and, under certain circumstances, white Americans.
- ✓ Racial profiling happens to both women and men, affects all age groups, is used against people from all socio-economic backgrounds, and occurs in rural, suburban and urban areas.
- ✓ Racial profiling of citizens and visitors of Middle Eastern and South Asian descent, and others who

Is Racial Profiling Justified?

"Do you think it is ever justified for police to use racial or ethnic profiling when stopping motorists on roads and highways?"

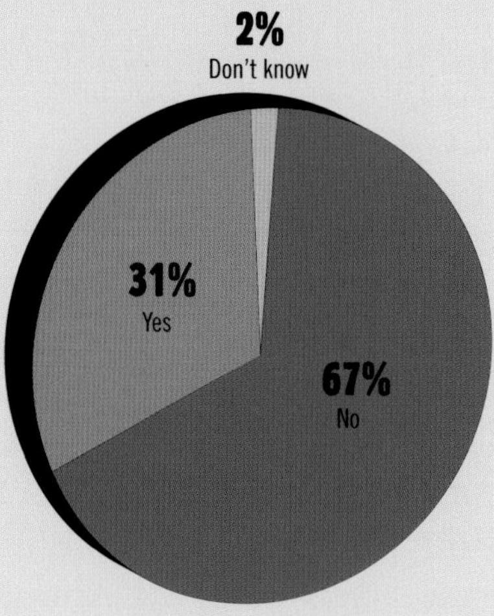

"Do you think it is ever justified for police to use racial or ethnic profiling when stopping passengers at security checkpoints in airports?"

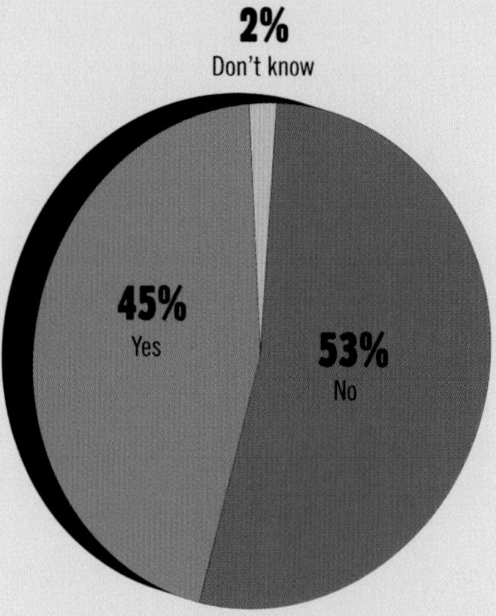

Polls taken June 2004; 2,250 total respondents
Source: The Gallup Organization

appear to be from these areas or members of the Muslim and Sikh faiths, has substantially increased since September 11, 2001.

Georgetown University law professor David Cole, the author of *No Equal Justice: Race and Class in the American Criminal Justice System*, says racial profiling violates a fundamental principle of American law: That individuals—not a specific class of people—are responsible for obeying the law. He writes, "Relying on race as a factor of suspicion violates the first principle of criminal law: individual responsibility. The state's authority to take citizens' liberty—and, in extreme cases, their lives—turns on the premise that all are equal before the law. Racial generalizations fail to treat people as individuals. As a result, policies that tolerate racial profiling undermine the criminal law's legitimacy."

5 RACISM IN THE POLICE FORCE

This video image shows Los Angeles police officers delivering a savage beating to Rodney King in March 1991. Police investigators later determined that the attack on King, a black man, was not racially motivated, although many Americans perceived the beating as an example of racially fueled police brutality.

Over and over again, the videotape played on news broadcasts. It was the spring of 1991 and Americans saw the beating of Rodney King countless times.

The King case unfolded in the early morning hours of March 3, 1991, when King led Los Angeles police on a high-speed chase. Once King finally stopped his car, he and his passengers were ordered out of the vehicle. Three white Los Angeles police officers then assaulted King, striking him with their batons 56 times. King was also kicked in the head and stunned with a Taser gun, which delivers a jolt of electrical current designed to momentarily incapacitate a suspect. He suffered a broken leg and multiple internal injuries and required hospitalization.

The assault was directed by a white police sergeant and witnessed by a dozen other police officers. It was also captured on videotape by an amateur photographer as well as on audio recordings made by dispatchers who recorded the chatter over their police radios. One officer said, "He pissed us off, so I guess he needs an ambulance now. . . . [S]hould know better than to run, they are going to pay a price when they do that." Another officer said, "I haven't beaten anyone this bad in a long time."

On March 20, just two weeks after the King beating, a Gallup poll reported that 92 percent of Americans had seen the videotape on television or had read about the incident in the news media. To the millions of Americans who watched at home, the Los Angeles police officers' assault on the hapless King revealed police brutality at its worst. What's more, 35 percent of respondents to the Gallup poll said they believed police brutality occurred in their own areas. As to the frequency of such incidents across the country, 22 percent of respondents said they occurred "very frequently," and 46 percent said "somewhat frequently." Alec M. Gallup observed:

> The incident in Los Angeles, in which a motorist was severely beaten by three police officers while a dozen others watched, seems to have caught the attention of the American public. Ninety-two percent say they saw or read about the beating, a very high awareness level for a local news event, and as many as two Americans in three (68%) believe that incidents of this kind occur very frequently or somewhat frequently across the country. . . .
>
> Nonwhites are more likely than whites to say that physical abuse by the police is frequent at both the national and local levels. More than three-quarters of nonwhites think incidents similar to the one in Los Angeles happen either very or somewhat frequently across the country, with four in ten claiming they happen very frequently. Four in ten say they happen very frequently or somewhat frequently in their own communities.

RACISM AND POLICE BRUTALITY

The videotape showing white policemen mercilessly beating a black man caused most people to conclude the assault was racially motivated. One person who drew this conclusion was Tom Bradley, the African-American mayor of Los Angeles. Shortly after the incident, Bradley told reporters, "It is no longer possible for any objective person to regard the King beating as an aberration. We must face the fact that there appears to be a dangerous trend of racially motivated incidents running through at least some segments of the Police Department." Civil rights leader Jesse Jackson and U.S. Representative Maxine Waters, an African-American member of Congress from Los Angeles, also accused the Los Angeles Police Department (LAPD) of racism.

Another observer who was convinced the assault was racially motivated was Tom Owens, a private detective and former Los Angeles police officer hired by Rodney King's attorney. Owens, who later wrote a book about the case, wrote, "Racism was at the very core of the incident."

In fact, the Los Angeles Police Department had been accused of racism many times in the past. For example, in 1988 Hall of Fame baseball player Joe Morgan was approached at Los Angeles International Airport by a plainclothes detective, accused of being a drug dealer, and roughed up. Morgan sued the city and won a settlement of nearly $800,000. In another case in 1983, a black off-duty suburban policeman named John Henry was stopped by two white LAPD officers while driving his family to visit a sick relative. Henry was pushed with a baton, handcuffed, and taken to jail. He sued, and won a $22,500 settlement. "It was overwhelming, to put it mildly," Henry said later. "I had taught my son to respect law enforcement, and for him to be trying to get out of the car to come and help me, that was bad."

And until 1983, Los Angeles police officers routinely employed chokeholds to subdue suspects. Applying the chokehold required the officer to wrap an arm around the suspect's throat and apply pressure. In some cases, the chokeholds were applied too tightly, resulting in suffocation, broken necks, and death. In 1982, it was revealed that over a seven-year period, 15 suspects had died from improperly applied chokeholds. Eleven were black. Wrote Tom Owens:

> I had used the chokehold many times while I was a cop. It was legal then, and my preferred method of controlling an unruly suspect. The chokehold was designed to cut off both the blood and air to a suspect's brain. The arrestee usually passed out and in the process of regaining consciousness, his or her body would twitch involuntarily. Sometimes they would lose control of their bodily functions. Officers dubbed these convulsions "the funky chicken." In the black humor of copdom,

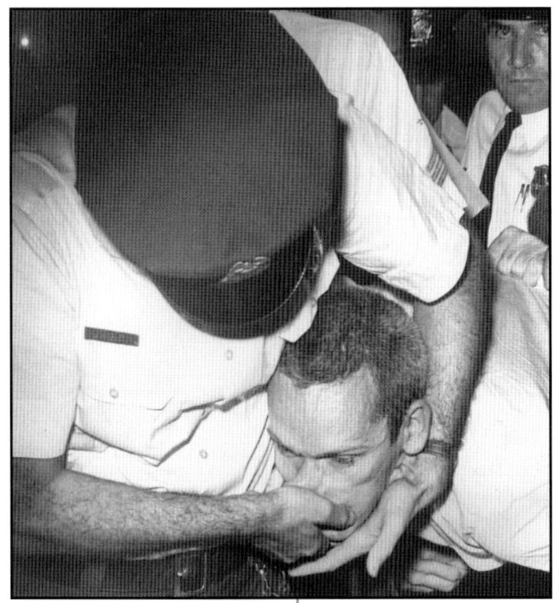

A Washington, D.C., policeman uses a chokehold to subdue a protestor during a 1962 civil rights demonstration. When applied with too much force, chokeholds can cause serious or fatal injuries, so they are rarely used today.

many officers rated performances of the funky chicken on a scale of one to ten for their entertainment value.

The chokehold was dropped as an acceptable police procedure when a black man, Adolph Lyons, sued the Los Angeles police after the chokehold had been applied to him when he was stopped for a routine traffic violation. The case was eventually argued before the U.S. Supreme Court. During the hearing, Supreme Court Justice Thurgood Marshall, the first African American to serve on the nation's highest court, interrupted the attorney presenting the LAPD's side of the case. Marshall asked, "Doesn't a loaded gun gain control? Why do you have to choke them to death?"

RACIST INTENT NOT CLEAR

Despite the pronouncement by Mayor Bradley and others that the assault on King had been racially motivated, the evidence would not present quite so clear a picture. As the investigation into the beating advanced, the LAPD's Internal Affairs detectives learned that two of the police officers involved in the incident, Timothy Wind and Theodore Briseno, never had been suspected of racially motivated violence in the past. As for Stacey Koon, the sergeant who directed the beating, the Internal Affairs detectives learned that he had once placed his own life at risk when he gave mouth-to-mouth resuscitation to a black man suspected of carrying the AIDS virus. But investigators also learned that the fourth officer involved in the King beating, Laurence Powell, had made a radio transmission shortly before the incident in which he referred to black suspects in an unrelated case as "gorillas."

When the text of Powell's radio transmission was reported in the press, many people formed the opinion that the beating of Rodney King actually was another racially motivated incident in a police department with too long a history of racially motivated beatings. Even many LAPD officers found themselves convinced of the racism within their ranks. Shortly after the King incident, the LAPD conducted its own poll of police officers to determine their attitudes toward the department's record on race-related brutality. According to the poll, 27.6 percent of police officers in the LAPD agreed with the statement "that an officer's prejudice toward the suspect's race may lead to the use of excessive force."

But as Internal Affairs investigators looked further into the case, they concluded the beating of King had not been racially motivated. King had been pulled over by police officers for reckless driving after speeding through residential neighborhoods at more than 100 miles per hour. The IA investigators learned that after police ordered King to step out of his car, the officers suspected he was high on PCP, a hallucinogenic drug that often prompts its users to display amazing feats of strength because it deadens their own feelings of pain. (It turned out that King had not been under the influence of PCP, although he had smoked marijuana before the chase.) As the incident unfolded, King fought hard against the officers, even breaking away from two of them and tossing them aside, then lunging toward Koon. "I knew if he gets hold of me and he grabs me in [the] neck . . . it's going to be a death grip, and you can have all 8,300 members of this police department pull this guy off and it's not going to work," Koon told the Internal Affairs investigators.

Despite the Internal Affairs investigators' conclusion that there was no racial intent in the King case, the investigators believed the officers had used excessive force in subduing King. Wind, Briseno, Powell, and Koon were ordered to face a criminal trial for participating in the assault.

ENDURING POLICE BRUTALITY

Police brutality in the United States has not been limited to the LAPD. In 1998, the international human-rights organization Human Rights Watch released a report on police brutality in the United States, in which it stated that race most definitely is a factor in incidents of excessive force by law enforcement officers. The report, titled *Shielded from Justice: Police Brutality,* said:

> Race continues to play a central role in police brutality in the United States. In the cities we have examined where such data are available, minorities have alleged human rights violations by police more frequently than white residents and far out of proportion to their representation in those cities. Police have subjected minorities to apparently discriminatory treatment and have physically abused minorities while using racial epithets. Mistreatment may be non-violent harassment and humiliation, such as allegations of racial profiling in which drivers are temporarily detained often for driving in certain areas or for driving certain cars. . . . Each new incident involving police mistreatment of an African American, Hispanic American or other minority—and particularly those that receive media attention—reinforce a general belief that some residents are subjected to particularly harsh treatment and racial bias.

Over the years, a significant number of black Americans have believed that minority members endure brutality by police. In 1969, for example, 39 percent of black respondents to a Gallup poll said they believe there is police brutality in their home towns. Thirty-seven percent of the respondents disagreed, but 22 percent said they were "not sure." Thirty years later, the Gallup Organization again polled on the issue of police brutality. This time, 43 percent of blacks said they felt they had been treated unfairly by the police because of their race. Overall, 38 percent of respondents of all races said they thought police brutality exists in their communities.

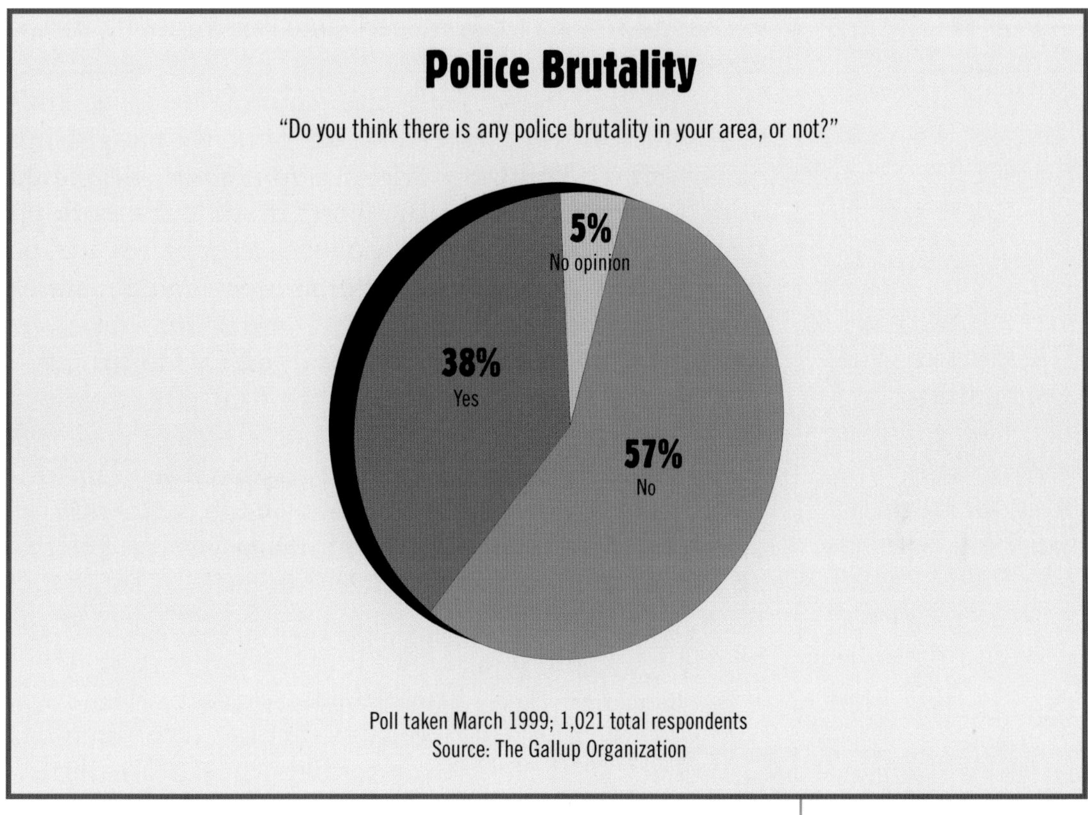

The 1999 Gallup poll was conducted a year after four white New York City police officers were indicted in the brutal beating of Abner Louima, a Haitian immigrant who was stopped by police outside a Brooklyn nightclub. The officers were alleged to have handcuffed and beaten Louima; one officer is said to have shoved a broom handle into Louima's rectum and mouth. Throughout the assault, two of the officers—Justin Volpe and Charles Schwarz—shouted racial slurs as they brutalized Louima. Volpe, the police officer alleged to have assaulted Louima with the broomstick, pleaded guilty and was sentenced to 30 years in prison. Schwarz was convicted and sentenced to 15 years in prison, but the verdict was later overturned on a technicality when he appealed. Schwarz eventually made a deal with prosecutors and agreed to plead guilty in exchange for a five-year sentence. Two other officers were acquitted.

In another New York case, four white New York City police officers were charged in the shooting death of Amadou Diallo, an African immigrant who died after being shot 41 times by police. In the early morning hours of February 4, 1999, police searching for a rape suspect had knocked on Diallo's door. When Diallo answered and was questioned about the rape, he reached inside his coat pocket and police opened fire.

A month after the shooting, the four police officers were indicted on charges of second-degree murder. A year later, they were acquitted by a jury, which included four black members. Attorneys for the police officers argued that it was dark in the doorway of Diallo's apartment and that the officers believed Diallo had been reaching for a gun. (Diallo had been reaching for his wallet when he was shot.)

An artist kneels near a memorial he painted in the Bronx honoring Amadou Diallo, an African immigrant who was mistakenly killed by New York police in 1999. The mural features police officers wearing Ku Klux Klan hoods.

Eric Adams, a black New York City police lieutenant who often has criticized his department's treatment of blacks, faulted the jury for not believing race was a significant issue in the case. "The jury stated from the onset that they didn't believe race had anything to do with this; they did not discuss race in the jury room," he said. "So regardless of what evidence was presented to not acknowledge that Amadou Diallo was shot and killed because he was a black man—that is clearly not looking at all the evidence."

Other cities have also endured racially motivated incidents of police brutality. The Human Rights Watch report cited incidents in 14 American cities in which blacks and Hispanics had been abused by police: Atlanta, Boston, Chicago, Detroit, Indianapolis, Minneapolis, New Orleans, Philadelphia, Providence, San Francisco, Washington, D.C., Los Angeles, New York, and Portland. As far back as 1968, the National Advisory Commission on Civil Disorders, which was impaneled by President Lyndon B. Johnson to investigate racial unrest and rioting in the cities, wrote:

> Almost invariably the incident that ignites disorder arises from police action. Harlem, Watts, Newark and Detroit—all the major outbursts of recent years—were precipitated by routine arrests of Negroes by white officers for minor offenses. . . . [T]o many Negroes police have come to symbolize white power, white racism and white repression. And the fact is that many police do reflect and express these white attitudes. The atmosphere of hostility and cynicism is reinforced by a widespread perception among Negroes of the existence of police brutality and corruption, and of a "double standard" or justice and protection—one for Negroes and one for whites.

Tom Owens, the former LAPD officer and detective in the Rodney King case, believes that most police officers accused of racism do not start out as racists. Instead, the pervasive police culture as well as their personal hatred of lawbreakers leads them to oversimplify the connection between race and crime. For example, a white police officer who may have grown up in a white, middle-class community where he experienced little crime suddenly finds himself assigned to a high-crime inner-city neighborhood populated by poor blacks and Hispanics. As a result, that officer may find himself concluding that blacks and Hispanics commit most crime.

"My experience has been that working in a predominantly black or disadvantaged community carries with it some unique problems," Owens said. "Already hardened by the influences of basic police training and street experience, an officer assigned to a minority area too often undergoes a transformation in attitude. More often than not, the officer will choose a stricter interpretation and a tougher course of action than he would in a 'better' neighborhood. Most African Americans have known this for years." Owens added that when he was on the police force, he often saw "no understanding, no compassion, no tolerance" by white officers for African Americans. He said, "This isn't to say that every cop working a minority area is a racist or abuser. But if one is heavy-handed and is not disciplined or retrained, that's one too many. He crosses the line—and the line is moved."

In the years that followed the incidents involving Rodney King, Abner Louima, and other minority victims, some cities established civilian review boards to oversee the police. In 1997, for instance, Pittsburgh voters passed a referendum that established the Citizen Police Review Board in their city. The board regularly holds public hearings on police brutality cases. By 2005, the board had investigated some 4,000 complaints filed by Pittsburgh residents, including more than 600 in which excessive force was alleged. Harry Liller, a Pittsburgh man whose sister was the victim of police brutality, told a reporter in 2005, "They at least bring light on these situations. They are doing what's right for the public."

And yet, brutality cases with racial overtones continue to make the news. One such incident occurred in 2005 when Palo Alto, California, police officers Michael Kan and Craig Lee, both Asian Americans, were tried on charges of beating Albert Hopkins, a 59-year-old black man. During testimony in the case, Hopkins insisted that he was victimized because he is black. The case ended in a mistrial when the jury deadlocked eight-to-four in favor of conviction. (Under law, all jury verdicts in criminal cases must be unanimous.) The four jurors who refused to vote for the convictions of Kan and Lee were Asian American. Sunday Udoffia, the lone black member of the jury, told a reporter, "I believe any police officer—whether you are black, white or Asian—if you do something wrong, you should be held accountable for your actions. I kept bringing that up to them: 'We're not looking at anybody's race here. We just want to make sure that this doesn't happen again.'"

DEEP FRUSTRATION AND ANGER

Following the Louima incident in New York, thousands of black citizens staged protests to demand that the rogue officers be brought to trial and that city officials crack down on racism in the police force. In the King case, racial tension in Los Angeles would build for more than a year, then explode into rioting following the trial of Wind, Powell, Briseno, and Koon. Due to excessive pre-trial publicity, attorneys for the policemen were able to move the trial to Simi Valley, a predominantly white community north of Los Angeles. In a verdict that stunned the nation, the all-white jury acquitted the four white defendants. In 1992, a Gallup poll found that 76 percent of Americans believed the verdict was not justified.

The verdict set off race riots in Los Angeles that resulted in the deaths of 54 people, injuries to 2,383 people, and the destruction of some $700 million in property. Police arrested 13,212 rioters. Violent protests in other cities broke out as well. A Gallup poll reported that nearly 70 percent of respondents agreed with the statement: "The riots in Los Angeles following the verdicts in the state court case are the result of the deep frustration and anger many blacks feel as a result of racial discrimination."

In an attempt to quell the violence, Los Angeles officials asked Rodney King to make a statement on national television, asking for a return to peace. Staring into the cameras, King made a plaintive plea to the nation:

Rodney King Verdict

"Do you think the verdict of 'not guilty' in the Rodney King case was justified or not justified?"

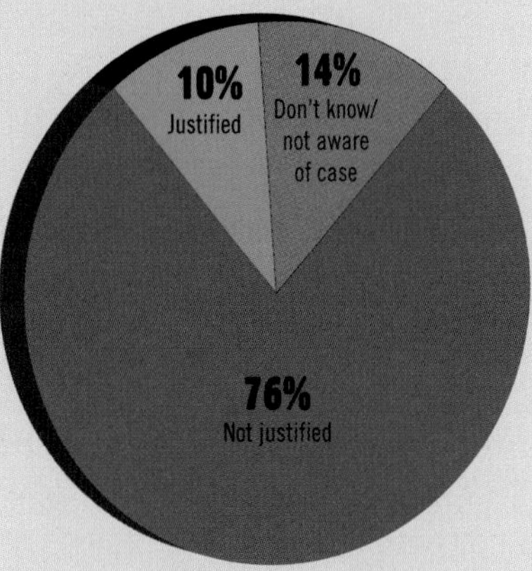

Poll taken April 1992; 1,930 total respondents
Source: The Gallup Organization

Los Angeles Riots

"Do you think that the riots in Los Angeles following the Rodney King case verdicts were the result of deep frustration and anger many blacks feel as a result of racial discrimination?"

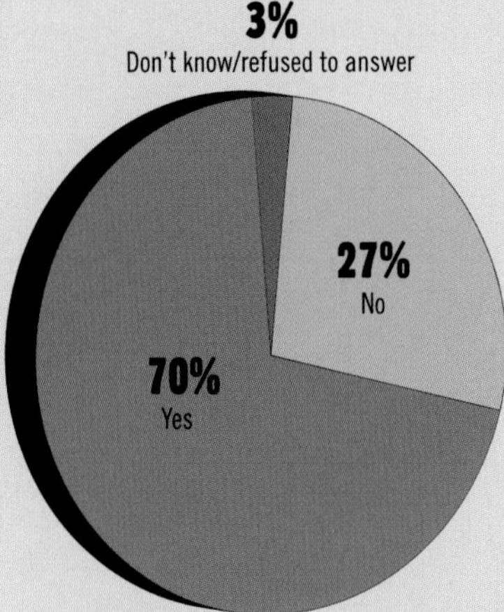

Poll taken February 1993; 840 total respondents
Source: The Gallup Organization

> Can we all get along? Can we stop making it horrible for the older people and the kids? We've got enough smog here in Los Angeles, let alone to deal with the setting of these fires and things. It's just not right. It's just not right, and it's not going to change anything. We'll get our justice. They've won the battle, but they haven't won the war. We will have our day in court, and that's all we want. I'm neutral, I love everybody. I love people of color. . . .
>
> We can all get along. We've just got to. Just got to. We're all stuck here for awhile. Let's try to work it out. Let's try to work it out.

A year after the acquittal in Simi Valley, the four officers were retried in federal court on the charge of violating Rodney King's civil rights. This time, a federal jury found two of the officers—Koon and Powell—guilty. Both were sentenced to jail terms. As for Rodney King, he would have his day in court as well. King sued the Los Angeles Police Department and was awarded a settlement of $3.8 million.

ARNOLD

6

THE DEBATE OVER AFFIRMATIVE ACTION

While hard-fought civil rights victories took place in the 1950s and 1960s, during the 1970s activists found Americans preoccupied with other pressing issues. In Washington, D.C., for example, the White House and Congress struggled to end American involvement in the Vietnam War. Soon after the American withdrawal, officials in the administration of President Richard M. Nixon found themselves awash in Watergate—the political scandal that eventually drove Nixon from office. Unrest in the Middle East caused oil prices to soar. Inflation hit the United States hard, causing a wave of massive unemployment. In Iran, anti-American sentiment hit a fever pitch in 1979 when Islamic fundamentalists stormed the U.S. Embassy in Tehran, taking fifty-two embassy workers hostage. The drama lasted 444 days as President Jimmy Carter found himself unable to win their freedom. And in Afghanistan, the former Soviet Union launched an invasion, prompting Carter to call for an American boycott of the 1980 Summer Olympics in Moscow.

Affirmative action was an important part of President Lyndon B. Johnson's domestic agenda. Johnson expanded on the original order issued by his predecessor, John F. Kennedy, with executive order 11246, issued in 1965 and later amended by executive order 11375. The order aims "to correct the effects of past and present discrimination" by prohibiting the federal government and its subcontractors from discriminating against anyone on the basis of race, skin color, religion, gender, or national origin.

As the 1980 presidential election approached, the preservation or expansion of civil rights seemed far from most people's minds. In September 1980, shortly before Carter and Republican presidential candidate Ronald Reagan held their only debate, a Gallup poll asked Americans to name the issues they wanted to see debated by the presidential contenders. The economy and foreign affairs dominated the poll; a mere 2 percent of the respondents said they hoped to hear the candidates talk about race relations and civil rights.

Reagan, the conservative former governor of California, won the election and brought about a dramatic change of direction in the federal government. He was elected on a pledge to slash federal spending, which he accomplished by scaling back Lyndon Johnson's Great Society anti-poverty programs, many of which benefited poor, inner-city blacks and Hispanics. State governments also grew conservative; many of them replaced "cradle to grave" welfare programs—which provided direct cash assistance to needy families—with so-called "workfare" programs, in which participants were guaranteed assistance for a limited time only and usually were required to provide labor for government-sponsored public works projects. After Reagan left office in 1989, this trend continued. In 1996, Congress passed a national welfare reform law, mandating a two-year limit on public assistance benefits for recipients and establishing rules that require many recipients to work in government-sponsored jobs. Shortly after the measure was passed, a Gallup poll showed that 68 percent of Americans favored the new law, with just 15 percent opposed.

With the gap growing between rich and poor, and with civil rights becoming less of a priority to lawmakers, it seemed as though the rights of minorities in the United States would erode. As the 20th century ended and a new century began, a civil rights concept from the 1960s would undergo new scrutiny: affirmative action.

ENHANCING EQUAL OPPORTUNITY

"Affirmative action" is a term used to describe policies or programs intended to provide advantages for people of a particular group. The intent of these programs is to reverse decades of discrimination and create a society in which people of all races enjoy equal social, political, and economic benefits.

Affirmative action in the United States dates back to March 6, 1961, when President Kennedy issued an executive order providing that government contractors "take affirmative action to ensure that applicants are employed, and employees are treated during employment, without regard to their race, creed, color, or national origin." Four years later, President Johnson issued an executive order prohibiting employment discrimination based on race, color, religion, and national origin by organizations receiving federal contracts. The order said:

President John F. Kennedy delivers the 1963 State of the Union message to Congress. Although Kennedy is generally seen as a supporter of civil rights for African Americans, most of the government programs he proposed, including affirmative action, were not fully implemented until after his assassination.

> The contractor will take affirmative action to ensure that applicants are employed, and that employees are treated during employment, without regard to their race, color, religion, sex or national origin. Such action shall include, but not be limited to the following: employment, upgrading, demotion, or transfer; recruitment or recruitment advertising; layoff or termination; rates of pay or other forms of compensation; and selection for training, including apprenticeship.

Johnson's goal was to enhance equal opportunity for women and minority members, but his executive order did not provide much guidance on how affirmative action was to be enacted. Still, given that discrimination was very much a problem in the 1960s, it was clear that steps had to be taken for the president's goals to be met.

SCHOOLS TAKE ACTION

While the executive orders called for affirmative action in the workplace, affirmative action occurred outside that sphere as well. During the 1960s, colleges, for example, looked at the compositions of their student bodies and realized that their students were mostly white and affluent. This meant that many blacks and other minorities were not receiving higher education. Also, though, colleges wondered what kind of education they were providing if most of their students were affluent and white. The only people their students would encounter during their college careers would be other affluent whites. And so, colleges sought to "diversify" their student bodies by aggressively recruiting minority members and offering them scholarships and other forms of aid that would finance their tuition, room and board, books, and other expenses.

Proponents of such programs argued that white students, as well as minorities, would benefit from greater minority enrollment in U.S. colleges. "Many educators have found anecdotal evidence that racial, ethnic, and gender diversity in collegiate settings helps to stimulate students' personal growth and intellectual development," states *How Affirmative Action Benefits America,* a report published by the American Psychological Association. Additionally, the report cites concrete data:

> In one of the most thorough studies of college student outcomes, psychologist Patricia Gurin found strong evidence that diversity in higher education settings yields important benefits for all students, including nonminorities. . . . Like many other psychologists, Gurin believes that exposure to the educational environment during late adolescence and early adulthood is important for enabling critical thinking, fostering participation in civil life and intellectual development that is deeper and involves more active mental alertness and problem solving. The opportunity for minority and nonminority students to interact with each other may foster this kind of intellectual development by exposing the students to alternative perspectives and cultural frameworks and by challenging students' assumptions.

With affirmative action plans in place, the ethnic makeup of student bodies started to change. In 1955—the year after the Supreme Court handed down the *Brown v. Board of Education* decision—less than 5 percent of American college students were black. By 1990, however, some 11 percent of college students were black—a percentage that more closely mirrored the overall African-American population in the United States.

Affirmative action wasn't only for black students. Statistics showed that between 1976 and 1993, the number of black students attending colleges rose by 36 percent. But statistics also showed that during the same period Asian American enrollment rose a dramatic 274 percent. At the same time, Hispanic students' enrollment rose by 160 percent and enrollment by Native Americans rose by nearly 62 percent. Clearly, colleges had made notable headway in diversifying their student bodies.

But what methods had colleges used to achieve such diversification? The Supreme Court first took up that issue in the 1970s. The case involved a prospective

Today, many experts believe that racial and ethnic diversity on college campuses helps both minority and non-minority students to develop creatively, socially, and intellectually.

medical student named Allan Paul Bakke who had sued the University of California at Davis, claiming he had twice been rejected for admission even though the university had accepted minority students with weaker academic records and lower test scores. Essentially, Bakke charged that he was the victim of reverse discrimination.

Bakke already had proven himself academically. Trained as an engineer, Bakke had been employed for six years by the National Aeronautics and Space Administration (NASA) when he decided to switch careers. The University of California admitted 100 students a year to the medical school at its Davis campus. Of those places, 16 slots were set aside as a quota for minority students. Bakke first applied for admission in 1973 and was rejected. He believed that he was qualified to attend the university but suspected that he had been passed over in favor of a minority student with lower test scores. In a letter to the admissions office when he resubmitted his application, Bakke wrote:

> Applicants chosen to be our doctors should be those presenting the best qualifications, both academic and personal. Most are selected according to this standard, but I am convinced that a significant fraction of every current medical class is judged by a separate criterion. I am referring to quotas, open or covert, for racial minorities. Medicine needs the ablest and most dedicated men in order to meet future health care needs. I realize that the rationale for these quotas is that they attempt to atone for past racial discrimination. But instituting a new racial bias, in favor of minorities, is just not a solution.

In his response to Bakke, Peter Storandt, the university's assistant dean for student affairs, acknowledged "a situation as painful for us as for you." While calling Bakke "remarkably able and well-qualified," the admissions officer, nevertheless, elected to reject his application a second time. As to Bakke's charge that the

An African-American woman holds a sign to protest during the Supreme Court's deliberations on the 1978 Bakke case. Ultimately, the Court decided that Bakke had been unfairly denied admission to the University of California Medical School.

university had instituted a quota system for minorities, Storandt acknowledged that the school actively recruited minority students. Said Storandt, "I don't know whether you would consider our procedure to have the overtones of a quota or not, certainly its design has been to avoid such designation, but the fact remains that most applicants to such a program are members of ethnic minority groups."

When the university rejected his application for the second time, Bakke filed a lawsuit arguing that he had been turned down for admission solely because of race. Ironically, Bakke alleged in his suit that the university had violated his rights under the Civil Rights Act of 1964—the law that was intended to provide equal opportunity for Americans in the minority.

SPLIT DECISION

The justices wrestled with the Bakke case for several months before finally issuing an order in June 1978. It was a split decision. Four justices agreed that Bakke had been unfairly denied admission to the university and called for the school to permit his entry into the medical school. Four justices disagreed, finding that the university's quota system represented a legitimate attempt to right the wrongs of the past. The tie was broken by Justice Lewis Powell Jr., who agreed that Bakke had been unfairly denied admission. On the strength of a 5-4 vote, Bakke won admission to medical school.

And yet, while Powell's decision struck down the university's minority recruitment plan, he did not disagree with the concept of affirmative action. Instead, he believed that a quota system was unconstitutional. He wrote: "Preferring members of any one group for no reason other than race or ethnic origin is discrimination for its own sake." Powell compared the University of California's minority recruitment plan with a similar plan employed by Harvard University. In Harvard's case, Powell wrote, the university had been able to diversify its student body, but without the need to resort to a quota system. He said, "The experience of other university admissions programs, which take race into account in achieving educational diversity valued by the First Amendment, demonstrates that the assignment of a fixed number of places to a minority group is not a necessary means toward that end."

Therefore, under the Supreme Court's order, universities were still free to pursue diversity in their student bodies—and, in fact, they were still permitted to take race into consideration as one of a number of factors in the admission process, as long as they did so on a case-by-case basis. However, they were specifically prohibited from designating a set number of slots in their classrooms for minority students. Quotas, the court ruled, were illegal.

A Gallup poll indicated that the public overwhelmingly supported Bakke in the case. In 1977—the year before the high court issued its verdict—81 percent of respondents told a Gallup poll that they opposed preferential treatment for minority members to make up for past discrimination. Just 11 percent of respondents favored preferential treatment. Similarly, a second Gallup poll indicated that most Americans did not believe affirmative action programs in schools and places of employment were necessary. A total of 67 percent of respondents agreed with the statement that "blacks have as good a chance as white people in your community to get any kind of job for which they are qualified," while just 24 percent of respondents disagreed. Further, 80 percent of respondents agreed with the statement "black children and other minorities in this community have the same educational opportunities as white children," while only 15 percent disagreed.

As for Allan Bakke, he entered medical school, graduated, and went on to pursue a successful career as a physician.

WINNERS AND LOSERS

The Bakke decision hardly laid to rest the issue of affirmative action as it applied both to college admissions and opportunities in the workplace. Following the decision, political scientists studied affirmative action's effects on U.S. society. Over the next two decades, conservatives and liberals debated the merits and flaws of affirmative action programs.

"Do you think that because of past discrimination women and members of minority groups should be given preferential treatment in getting jobs and places in college instead of decisions based on their ability?"

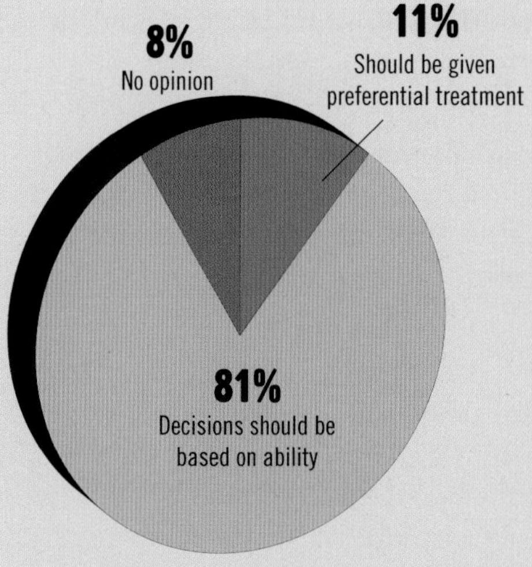

Poll taken October 1977; 2,658 total respondents
Source: The Gallup Organization

Conservatives argued that even without a quota system, affirmative action gave an unfair advantage to minorities—particularly in business and other workplaces. They claimed that the tradition in the United States had been to reward the employee who works hardest, who brings the most talent to the job, and who produces the best results. Under the free enterprise system, the contractor who submits a bid to do a job the fastest and for the least amount of money usually is rewarded by winning the contract. But under affirmative action, it seemed to many conservatives that minorities wouldn't have to do their best, or work their hardest, or possess the most talent, or bid the lowest to get a job. Commenting on a case in which a state government enlisted an affirmative action officer to help award human services contracts to minority-owned companies, conservative writer Arch Puddington wrote in a 1998 issue of the magazine *Commentary*:

> In almost every instance, there are winners and losers. The winners are the undeserving agencies that win contract awards, and the diversity officials who take credit for "expanding opportunity" to minorities. The losers are the agencies that were passed over, despite their superior performance, and the social-service clients who are likely to receive subpar services. Some of the agencies passed over are large enough and wealthy enough to sustain the setback with no serious consequences; others, however, are small operations run by highly motivated and extraordinarily hard-working professionals. The loss of a major contract can mean a great deal to these smaller agencies.

Meanwhile, liberal politicians and commentators and civil rights activists argued that although affirmative action was not a perfect system, it nevertheless served an important purpose in the United States. The noted African-American scholar and activist Cornel West pointed out in his 1993 book *Race Matters* that often in American history there had been government-sponsored "redistributive measures," which made benefits available to people who were members of social classes that had previously been denied fair treatment. He noted that immigrants had been granted favors in the form of loans, contracts, and jobs by political bosses who needed their votes. For years, he said, farmers were paid subsidies to ensure their crops would return profits. In addition, he said, soldiers returning from wars were often granted benefits such as subsidized college tuition to reward them for their service to the country.

West also saw affirmative action as an effective mechanism working against racism. He argued that without the safeguard of affirmative action in place, jobs and educational opportunities reserved for minorities would quickly disappear. In *Race Matters*, he wrote:

> Progressives should view affirmative action as neither a major solution to poverty nor a sufficient means to equality. We should see it as primarily playing a negative role—namely, to ensure that discriminatory practices against women and people of color are abated. Given the history of this country, it is a virtual certainty that without affirmative action racial and sexual discrimination would return with a vengeance. Even if affirmative action fails significantly to reduce black poverty or contributes to the persistence of racist perceptions in the workplace, without affirmative action black access to America's prosperity would be even more difficult to obtain and racism in the workplace would persist anyway.

TWO-TRACK SYSTEM UNFAIR

While the debate raged, new challenges to affirmative action started making their way through state legislatures and federal courts. It appeared as though opponents were finding ways to whittle away at the core concept of affirmative action, as described in the Bakke decision. In 1995, for instance, the U.S. Supreme Court ruled that college-financed scholarships cannot be reserved strictly for minorities. The court also issued a decision that year finding that in some cases, minority contractors had to prove they had been victims of discrimination in order to take advantage of affirmative action benefits.

That same year, the University of California—whose quota system had sparked the Bakke decision—abolished all preferential treatment for minorities seeking admission. Later, California Governor Pete Wilson signed into law legislation authorized under Proposition 209, a public referendum adopted by voters in 1996. Proposition 209 declared that the state government should "not discriminate against, or grant preferential treatment to, any individual or group on the basis of race, sex, color, ethnicity, or national origin in the operation of public employment, public education, or public contracting."

In 1996, the Supreme Court sharply rebuked one college for its affirmative action program. The court reviewed a lawsuit brought against the law school of the University of Texas by Cheryl Hopwood, who had

Young people protest against Proposition 209, the 1996 California ballot initiative that banned affirmative action programs at all state institutions. In the first few years after the initiative was passed, enrollment of African American, Hispanic, and Native American students plunged throughout the University of California system, although the enrollment of Asian Americans continued to rise.

been turned down for admission to the school even though she carried a 3.8 average (out of 4.0) through college and scored in the top 17 percent of students who took the law school admissions examination. Hopwood charged that the law school actually had employed color-coding on applications, indicating which applications were submitted by black and Hispanic students. Hopwood argued that her test scores and grade-point average were higher than all but three of the 50 Hispanic students and all but one of the 25 black students who were accepted instead of her. After hearing the case, the Supreme Court ruled that a "two-track" admissions system that treats the races differently is unfair. Still, the high court did not totally toss out affirmative action, ruling that race could still be regarded as a "plus factor" in college admissions.

Nevertheless, a year after the Hopwood decision, Hispanic enrollment at the University of Texas law school dropped by 64 percent, while black enrollment dropped by 88 percent. And in California, enactment of Proposition 209 resulted in a drop in minority enrollment at many of the University of California's campuses. For example, at the Berkeley campus, minority enrollment dropped by half. Law school admissions throughout the California state university system saw a 72 percent decrease in black students and a 35 percent decrease in Hispanic students.

In 1997, the fight against affirmative action would be taken up by Jennifer Gratz and Patrick Hamacher, who had been turned down for admission as undergraduates at the University of Michigan. They filed suit against the school, contending that their rejections were based solely on race. In their case, the two students alleged that the university's College of Literature, Science, and Arts maintained a point system when assessing potential students. Under the system, a potential student needed at least 100 out of a maximum of 150 points to be admitted. However, attorneys for Gratz and Hamacher alleged, the university automatically gave blacks, Hispanics, and other minority students 20 points based on their race or ethnic backgrounds.

A separate case against the University of Michigan also was filed that year. In that case, Barbara Grutter, a 48-year-old Michigan woman, alleged that she had been denied admission to the university's law school on the basis of race. In the Grutter case, attorneys did not cite a point system or some other method of specifically giving an advantage to a prospective minority student. Instead, her attorneys called into question the whole concept of affirmative action, in an attempt to overturn the court's decision in the Bakke case.

The cases moved slowly through the courts. Finally, in 2003 the U.S. Supreme Court heard arguments on the University of Michigan cases. As the justices mulled over their decision and affirmative action was debated in the media, Gallup polls showed that Americans' support for affirmative action was rising. In a Gallup Social Audit of Race Relations released in April 2003, two months before the Supreme Court issued its decision in the University of Michigan cases, 37 percent of respondents said they believe society should maintain the level of affirmative action offered in schools and places of employment, while 28 percent of Americans said they favor an increase in affirmative action programs. A Gallup analysis pointed out that white respondents in the poll showed a new enthusiasm for affirmative action—40 percent of whites said the level of affirmative action should be kept the same, while 22 percent called for an increase in affirmative action programs. The poll also found that 28 percent of whites and 8 percent of blacks favored a decrease in affirmative action programs. According to a Gallup analysis:

> The most recent results reveal a shift in white Americans' opinions, suggesting some narrowing of the familiar racial division on this issue. For the first time

since Gallup began asking this question in 1995, a clear plurality of whites (40%) say they would like to keep affirmative action programs at their current level. And although the percentage of whites who would like to see a decrease in affirmative action (28%) is much higher than the corresponding percentage among blacks, it is at its lowest level since 1995. Whether this movement toward greater acceptance of affirmative action corresponds with increased public support for specific affirmative action policies, such as the one under review at the University of Michigan, is not clear. . . . [H]istorical Gallup data indicate that while majorities of both black Americans and white Americans support affirmative action programs that encourage the hiring and admissions of minorities, clear majorities of both groups oppose policies that involve "lowering standards in order to make up for past discrimination." However, in

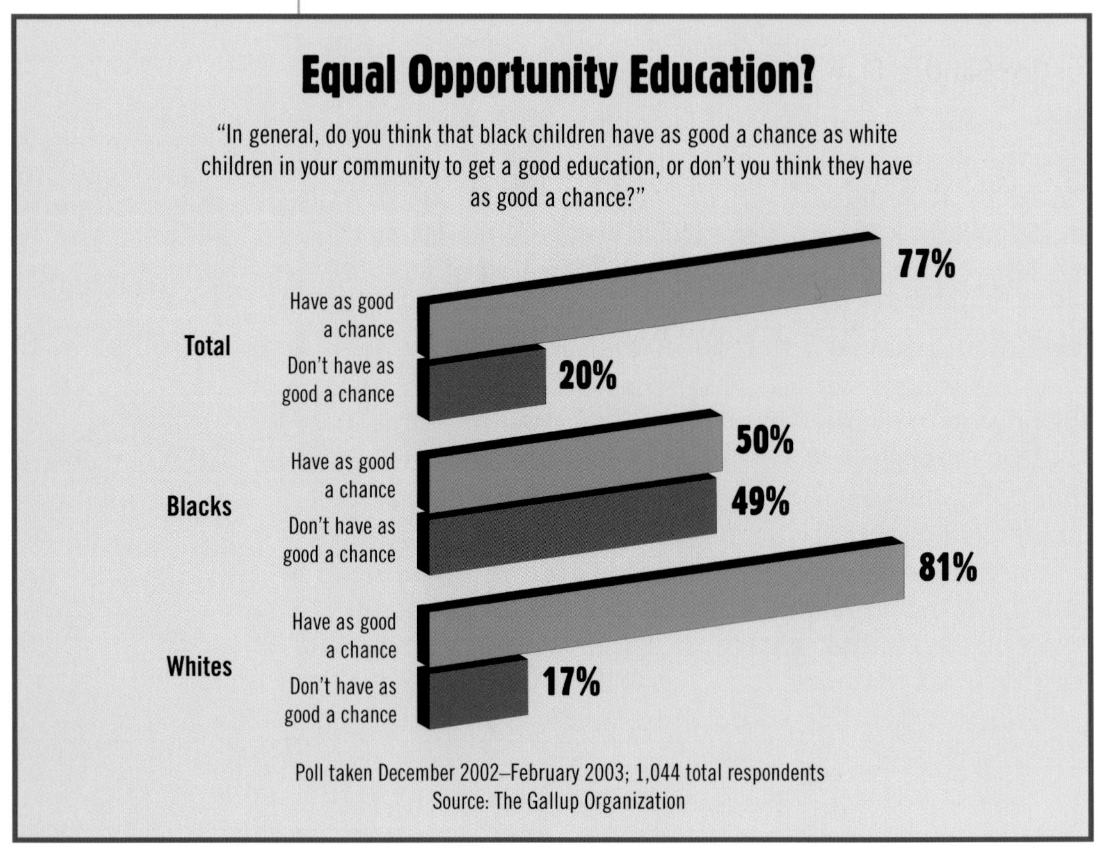

the warming climate of acceptance toward affirmative action, Michigan's argument that its policy is not just aimed at correcting past discrimination, but is a proactive measure to improve diversity on campus, might receive a more favorable public reaction than it would have in the past.

As in Bakke, the court issued a split decision in the Michigan case. Once again, the Supreme Court upheld affirmative action, ruling that a university could regard race as a factor in its effort to diversify its student body. However, the point system employed by the University of Michigan for undergraduate admissions was found to be unconstitutional. As in the University of Texas case involving Cheryl Hopwood, the court found that no separate system could be employed to reward students based on their ethnic backgrounds.

Nevertheless, in the majority opinion, authored by Justice Sandra Day O'Connor, the high court declared that diversity on college campuses remains an important national goal and that colleges should be encouraged to recruit students of many races. O'Connor wrote, "In order to cultivate a set of leaders with legitimacy in the eyes of the citizenry, it is necessary that the path to leadership be visibly open to talented and qualified individuals of every race and ethnicity."

7 THE ELUSIVE GOAL OF RACIAL EQUALITY

A group of high-school students eat lunch in their school's cafeteria. Fifty years after the landmark *Brown v. Board of Education* decision, many schools are becoming resegregated for economic reasons.

A study by Harvard University shows that more than five decades after *Brown v. Board of Education* desegregated schools, the hard-fought gains in civil rights for minorities have been eroding. The study, titled *Resegregation in American Schools* and released in 1999, addressed the concept known as "resegregation"—the return to a system of segregated schools.

The authors found that in 1998, 36 percent of black students attended schools where the black enrollment was more than 90 percent—a 4 percent rise since 1986. Meanwhile, the study said, 37 percent of Hispanic students attended schools in 1998 where the minority enrollment was more than 90 percent, a 14 percent rise since 1968.

The return to segregation did not occur because of a revival of Jim Crow laws but because of what the authors called "concentrated poverty"—a situation in which many minorities remain poverty-stricken and stuck in poor inner cities or rural regions, while white families have fled to affluent suburbs. According to the study:

> Though we usually think of segregation in racial and ethnic terms, it's important to also realize that the spreading segregation has a strong class component. When African-American and Latino students are segregated into schools where the majority of students are non-white, they are very likely to find themselves in schools where poverty is concentrated. This is of course not the case

> with segregated white students, whose majority-white schools almost always enroll high proportions of students from the middle class. This is a crucial difference, because concentrated poverty is linked to lower educational achievement. School level poverty is related to many variables that [affect] a school's overall chance at successfully educating students, including parent education levels, availability of advanced courses, teachers with credentials in the subject they are teaching, instability of enrollment, dropouts, unrelated health problems, lower college-going rates and many other important factors.

Following the release of the report, journalists started looking at schools in local communities to see if they were falling into a pattern of resegregation. One of the places where they found resegregation was Little Rock, Arkansas—the city where the line had been drawn against school desegregation in 1957. In Little Rock, whites make up 55 percent of the population while blacks compose 40 percent. Yet at Little Rock schools blacks make up 70 percent of the student body, because white parents in Little Rock have been taking their students out of the public schools and sending them to affluent suburban school districts or expensive private schools. Ann Marshall, head of the Office of Desegregation Monitoring, a federal court office that oversees integration in Little Rock schools, told a news reporter, "People with the means to opt out, if they think for any reason that the schools are unsavory, they do so. Then you have a decline in resources."

GOALS NOT MET

The resegregation of schools provides evidence that a half-century after *Brown v. Board of Education,* racial equality in the United States remains an elusive goal. In 2003, a Gallup poll found that half of all Americans believe either "all or most" of the goals of the 1960s civil rights movement have been accomplished. Still,

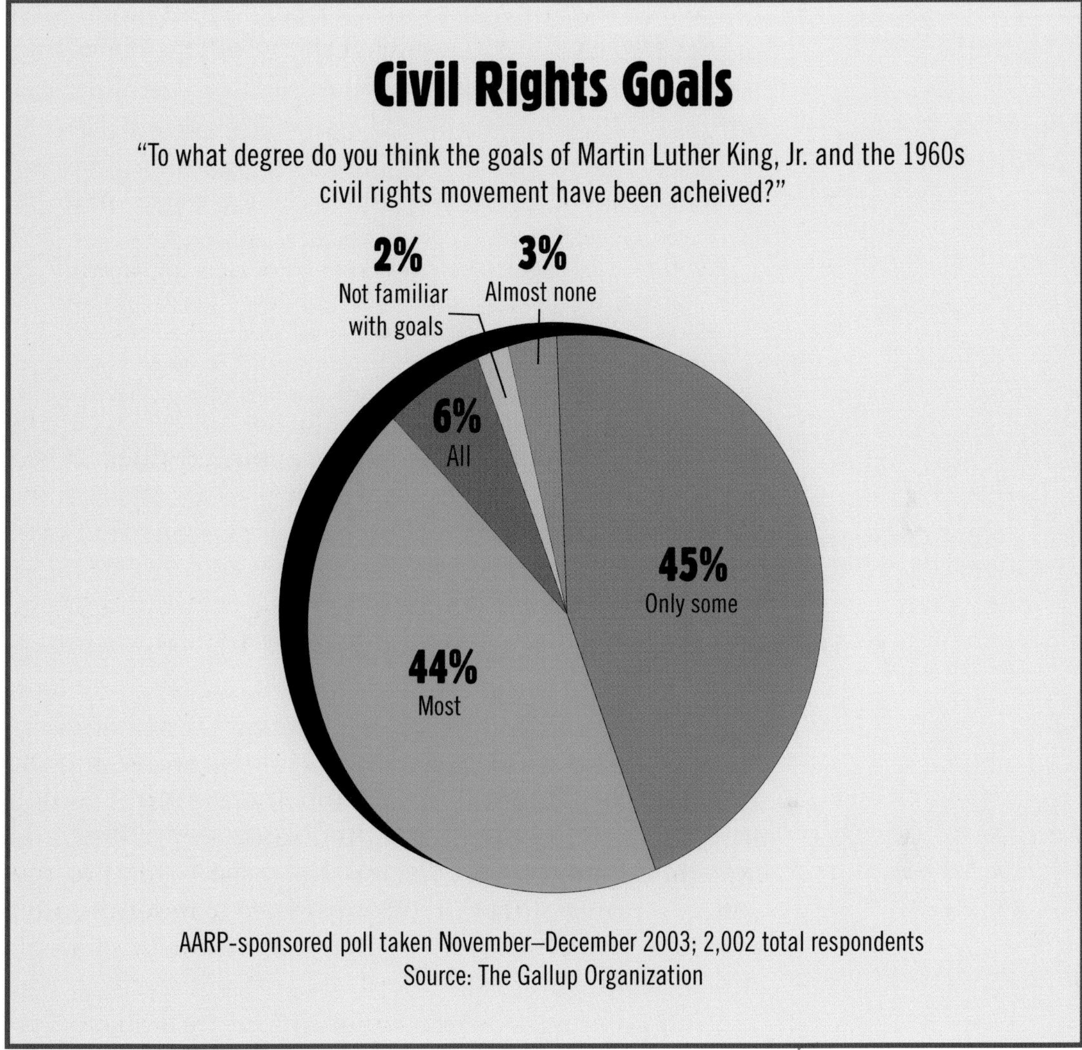

45 percent of Americans believe that "only some" civil rights goals have been met, while 3 percent believe "almost none" of the goals have been met. When respondents were categorized by race, the poll found more whites than minorities believing civil rights goals have been accomplished: Fifty-six percent of whites feel all or most goals have been achieved, while just 38 percent of Hispanics and 21 percent of blacks believe they have been achieved.

One of the chief victories of the equality movement in the 1960s was adoption of the Civil Rights Act of 1964, which provided the federal courts with jurisdiction over discrimination cases and authorized the U.S. Justice Department to defend the rights of Americans who feel they have been denied equal protection under the law. According to a 2004 Gallup analysis of the 2003 poll:

> While the goals of the law are clear, unequal treatment of blacks and other minorities continues to be an issue in American society 40 years after its enactment. While Americans believe that important progress has been made, black and Hispanic minorities still feel discriminated against in daily life, in many of the settings detailed in the Civil Rights Act.

HOPE FOR THE FUTURE

Still, there is hope. While many Americans remain doubtful about the success of the civil rights movement, the Gallup poll found that 81 percent of respondents believe the movement was either "extremely important" or "very important" to the United States. The poll reported that Americans still endorse civil rights and that they believe equality for the races is vital to the nation's future. Overall, 62 percent of Americans said the civil rights movement is "broadly beneficial" to all Americans.

And so, it is clear that most Americans believe that the fight was worth fighting. Over the past century, many Americans sacrificed and suffered for equality. They include the Japanese Americans who endured internment during World War II and the Hispanics who suffered as fruit growers took advantage of bracero labor. They include the members of the Little Rock Nine, who had to attend high school under the most difficult of circumstances. And there were those who made the ultimate sacrifice—the blacks who lost their lives in lynchings; civil rights workers like Michael

Schwerner, Andrew Goodman, and James Chaney, who were murdered by segregationists; and the movement's greatest leader, Martin Luther King Jr., assassinated because he spoke up for equality and justice.

The civil rights movement will continue into the 21st century. Although there have been setbacks such as economic segregation, history shows that the American people possess a hard resolve and will overcome. "This is our hope. This is the faith with which I return to the South," the Reverend King said in 1963, and his optimism still inspires. "With this faith we will be able to hew out of the mountain of despair a stone of hope. With this faith we will be able to transform the jangling discords of our nation into a beautiful symphony of brotherhood. With this faith we will be able to work together, pray together, to struggle together, to go to jail together, to stand up for freedom together, knowing that we will be free one day."

affirmative action—a term used to describe policies or programs intended to provide advantages for people of a particular racial group. The intent of affirmative action programs is to reverse past discrimination and create a society in which people of all races enjoy equal social, political, and economic benefits.

anti-miscegenation laws—laws that prevent two people of different racial backgrounds from marrying.

boycott—political statement made by refusing to take part in an otherwise normal delivery of services or products.

busing—practice of desegregating schools by transporting by bus students of one ethnicity to neighborhood schools dominated by populations of other ethnicities.

conservative—political movement whose leaders preach a cautious approach to change.

fundamentalists—people that adhere to a literal interpretation of their religious or political doctrines.

internment—imprisonment, usually of enemy aliens.

lawsuit—document containing charges brought in civil court.

liberal—political movement whose leaders endorse progress and change.

plank—principle outlined by a political organization, usually included in a party platform.

prejudice—an unfounded hatred, fear, or mistrust of a particular person because he or she is a member of a particular racial, ethnic, religious, or national group.

quota—percentage or share of a total made up of specific people or items, often established by rule or policy.

racial profiling—a practice in which police officers regard members of minority groups as suspects in criminal activities simply on the basis of their race.

racism—a belief that people of different races have different qualities and abilities, and that certain races are inherently superior or inferior; this belief is usually accompanied by prejudice or animosity against people who belong to other racial groups.

Reconstruction—period following the Civil War (1865–1876) in which the Southern states were reintegrated into the Union.

referendum—public ballot in which voters are given the opportunity to state their preferences on an issue; the outcome is often binding on the government.

segregation—the practice of keeping ethnic, racial, religious, or gender groups separate, often through use of separate schools, forms of public transportation, housing, and other facilities.

FURTHER READING

Bell, Derrick. *Silent Covenants: Brown v. Board of Education and the Unfulfilled Hopes for Racial Reform.* New York: Oxford University Press USA, 2004.

Burris, John L. *Blue vs. Black: Let's End the Conflict Between Cops and Minorities.* New York: St. Martin's Press, 1999.

Cole, David. *No Equal Justice: Race and Class in the American Criminal Justice System.* New York: The New Press, 2005.

Curry, George E., ed. *The Affirmative Action Debate.* Boston: Addison Wesley Publishing Company, 1996.

Harris, David A. *Profiles in Injustice: Why Racial Profiling Cannot Work.* New York: W. W. Norton & Company, 2003.

King, Martin Luther Jr., and Clayborne Carson. *The Autobiography of Martin Luther King Jr.* New York: Warner Books, 2001.

Laird, Bob. *The Case for Affirmative Action in University Admissions.* Berkeley, Calif.: Bay Tree Publishing, 2005.

Matthiessen, Peter. *Sal Si Puedes: Cesar Chavez and the New American Revolution.* New York: Random House, 1969.

Wu, Frank H. *Yellow: Race in America Beyond Black and White.* New York: Basic Books, 2002.

BOOKS AND PERIODICALS

"After the Verdict," PBS NewHour, March 3, 2000, www.pbs.org/newshour/bb/law/jan-june00/diallo_3-3.html

Bass, Patrick Henry. *Like a Mighty Stream: The March on Washington.* Philadelphia: Running Press, 2002.

"Black Leaders Denounce White Senator's Racist Remarks," *Jet*, Jan. 6, 2003.

Cannon, Lou. *Official Negligence: How Rodney King and the Riots Changed Los Angeles and the LAPD.* New York: Times Books, 1997.

"Census Figures Show Dramatic Growth in Asian, Hispanic Populations," CNN, Aug. 30, 2002, www.cnnstudentnews.com/2000/US/08/30/minority.population/

The Civil Rights Movement. Pasadena, Calif.: Salem Press, 2000.

Cole, David. "Unequal Justice," *Baltimore Sun*, May 16, 1999, reprinted in Louise I. Gerdes, editor, *Police Brutality: Current Controversies*, Farmington Hills, Mich.: Greenhaven Press, 2004.

Crabtree, Steve. "Bakke and Affirmative Action," Gallup Organization, Jan. 28, 2003.

Drew, Kevin. "Today's Battle in the Classrooms: Resegregation," CNN.com/2004/LAW/05/15/schools.desegregation/

Dreyfuss, Joel, and Charles Lawrence III. *The Bakke Case: The Politics of Inequality.* New York: Harcourt Brace & Jovanovich, 1979.

Dunne, John Gregory. *Delano: The Story of the California Grape Strike.* New York: Farrar, Straus and Giroux, 1967.

Ferriss, Susan, and Ricardo Sandoval. *The Fight in the Fields: Cesar Chavez and the Farmworkers Movement.* New York: Harcourt Brace and Co., 1997.

Gallup, Alec M. "Americans Say Police Brutality Frequent—But Not Locally," Gallup Poll News Service, March 20, 1991.

Gathright, Alan. "Police Beating Case Ends in a Mistrial—Jury Deadlocked, 8 on Panel Favored Convicting Palo Alto Officers of Brutality," *San Francisco Chronicle*, April 19, 2005, http://sfgate.com/cgi-bin/article.cgi?file=/c/a/2005/04/19/PALO.TMP

Goldberg, Jeffrey. "The Color of Suspicion," *New York Times Sunday Magazine*, June 20, 1999.

Goodgame, Dan, and Karen Tumulty. "Tripped Up by History, Leader Trent Lott's Remarks on Race Raise a Storm and a Hot Question: Can Republicans Really Outgrow Their Past?" *Time*, vol. 160, no. 26, December 23, 2002.

Greenhouse, Linda. "Justices Back Affirmative Action by 5 to 4, but Wider Vote Bans a Racial Point System," *New York Times*, June 24, 2003.

Halberstam, David. *The Fifties*. New York: Villard Books, 1993.

Harris, David A. *Profiles in Injustice: Why Racial Profiling Cannot Work*. New York: The New Press, 2002.

Hayes, Stephen F. "Trent Lott Apologizes, Over and Over," *Weekly Standard*, Dec. 23, 2002.

Knowles, John, Nicola Persico, and Petra Todd. "Racial Bias in Motor Vehicle Searches: Theory and Evidence," *Journal of Political Economy*, vol. 109, no. 11, 2001.

Ludwig, Jack. "Has the Civil Rights Movement Overcome?" Gallup Organization, June 8, 2004.

———. "Public Warming to Affirmative Action as Supreme Court Hears Michigan Case," Gallup Organization, April 1, 2003.

Lyons, Lynda. "The Darkest Hours of Racial Unrest," Gallup Organization, June 3, 2003.

Orfield, Gary, and John T. Yun. *Resegregation in American Schools*. Cambridge, Mass.: The Civil Rights Project, Harvard University, 1999.

Owens, Tom, and Rod Browning. *Lying Eyes: The Ruth Behind the Corruption and Brutality of the LAPD and the Beating of Rodney King*. New York: Thunder's Mouth Press, 1994.

Puddington, Arch. "Affirmative Action Does Not Promote Equality," *Commentary*, 1998, reprinted in *Work: Opposing Viewpoints*. San Diego: Greenhaven Press, 2002.

"Racial Profiling," PBS NewsHour, March 13, 2001, www.pbs.org/newshour/bb/race_relations/jan-june01/profiling_3-13.htm

Ray, Julie. "Reflections on the 'Trouble in Little Rock,' Part I," Gallup Organization, Feb. 25, 2003.

———. "Reflections on the 'Trouble in Little Rock,' Part II" Gallup Organization, March 4, 2003.

Savage, David. "Court Lets Stand Ruling Against Race Preference," *Los Angeles Times*, July 2, 1996.

Schott, Richard G. "The Role of Race in Law Enforcement: Racial Profiling or Legitimate Use?" *FBI Law Enforcement Bulletin*, Nov. 1, 2001.

Searle, Clayton. "Profiling in Law Enforcement," International Narcotics Interdiction Association, www.inia.org/whats-new-presidents.htm

Silver, Jonathan D. "City's Citizen Police Review Board Still a Subject for Debate," *Pittsburgh Post-Gazette*, May 3, 2005, www.post-gazette.com/pg/05123/498068.stm

Toby, Jackson. "Racial Profiling Doesn't Prove Cops Are Racist," *Wall Street Journal*, March 11, 1999.

Twain, Mark. *Roughing It: California as I Saw It*, http://memory.loc.gov/ammem/ndlpedu/features/timeline/riseind/chinimms/twain.html

Weisner, Stephen G., and William F. Hartford, eds. A*merican Portraits: Biographies in United States History*. Boston: McGraw-Hill, 1998.

West, Cornel. *Race Matters*. Boston: Beacon Press, 1993.

Wormser, Richard. *The Rise and Fall of Jim Crow.* New York: St. Martin's Press, 2003.

INTERNET REPORTS

Boyd, Donald, *statement on racial profiling*, Amnesty International USA, www.amnestyusa.org/racial_profiling/document.do?id=4E41227CC1B49E4A85256F10005F5AEB.

A Brief History of Affirmative Action, Office of Equal Opportunity and Diversity, University of California, Irvine, www.eod.uci.edu/aa.html.

Exhibit: Eleanor Roosevelt Letter, National Archives and Records Administration, www.archives.gov/exhibit_hall/american_originals/eleanor.html.

How Affirmative Action Benefits America, American Psychological Association, Office of Public Communications, Washington, DC, August 1999.

National Drug Intelligence Center, Maryland Drug Threat Assessment, August 2002, www.usdoj.gov/ndic/pubs1/1827/overview.htm.

Shielded From Justice: Police Brutality, Human Rights Watch, July 1998, www.hrw.org/about/initiatives/police.htm.

Skyline Drive Historic District Boundary Increase, U.S. Department of Interior, National Park Service, www.nps.gov/shen/CR/pdf/NR_Form_Sec%208.doc.pdf.

Threat and Humiliation: Racial Profiling, National Security, and Human Rights in the United States, Amnesty International USA, September 2004, www.amnestyusa.org/racial_profiling/report/index.html.

EXPLORING THE JAPANESE AMERICAN INTERNMENT

www.jainternment.org

Sponsored by the National Asian American Telecommunications Association, the web page provides photographs and narratives of the period in American history in which innocent American citizens were held in camps because the government suspected they would spy or act as saboteurs for an enemy nation.

THE GALLUP ORGANIZATION

www.gallup.com

The website of the national polling institute includes polling data and analyses on hundreds of topics.

NATIONAL ARCHIVES AND RECORDS ADMINISTRATION

www.archives.gov/exhibit_hall/american_originals/eleanor.html

As part of the agency's on-line American Originals series, one can read Eleanor Roosevelt's letter to the Daughters of the American Revolution protesting the exclusion of Marian Anderson from Constitution Hall; other documents from the Anderson case, as well as a narrative of the controversy, are available as well.

RESEGREGATION IN AMERICAN SCHOOLS

www.civilrightsproject.harvard.edu

The report written by the Civil Rights Project at Harvard University can be downloaded at this Internet site.

SANFRANCISCOCHINATOWN.COM

www.sanfranciscochinatown.com/history/index.html

The history of Chinese immigration in America is chronicled on this Web page sponsored by SanFranciscoChinatown.com, a project of the Chinese-American community of the San Francisco area.

SHIELDED FROM JUSTICE

www.hrw.org/about/initiatives/police.htm

Shielded from Justice, the report that chronicles cases of police brutality in the United States, can be downloaded at this site maintained by Human Rights Watch.

U.S. SUPREME COURT

www.supremecourtus.gov

By entering "race" into the search engine of the U.S. Supreme Court's Internet page, students can access dozens of briefs, decisions, and other documents indicating the court's perspectives on equality.

"ZOOT SUIT RIOTS"

www.pbs.org/wgbh/amex/zoot/

A companion web page to a PBS documentary on the riots that targeted Hispanic citizens living in Los Angeles during the 1940s.

AMERICAN CIVIL LIBERTIES UNION
125 Broad Street, 18th Floor
New York, NY 10004
212 549-2585
Website: www.aclu.org

The ACLU has a long history of defending civil rights in the courts; visitors to the organization's website can find updates on many ACLU cases and projects by following the "racial justice" link.

AMNESTY INTERNATIONAL USA
5 Penn Plaza 14th Floor
New York, NY 10001
212 807-8400
Website: www.amnestyusa.org

The mission of Amnesty International USA is to expose violations of human rights; among the group's projects is a campaign against racial profiling.

DAUGHTERS OF THE AMERICAN REVOLUTION
Library and Museum
1776 D Street, NW
Washington, D.C. 20006-5303
202 628-1776
Website: www.dar.org

The organization, composed of descendants of Revolutionary War veterans, maintains a museum and library in Washington, D.C., and has resources available on its Internet page for the student seeking information about Marian Anderson and the DAR's refusal to permit her to sing in Constitution Hall.

SOUTHERN POVERTY LAW CENTER
400 Washington Avenue
Montgomery, AL 36104
334 956-8200
Website: www.splcenter.org

The organization gathers intelligence on the growth of hate groups in the United States. It issues regular reports, and has initiated lawsuits against groups that seek to oppress the rights of minority groups.

U.S. CENSUS BUREAU
4700 Silver Hill Road
Washington DC 20233-0001
301 763-INFO
Website: www.census.gov

The agency charged with charting the growth of population in the United States has developed many reports on race in America; students can access data on race by going to the "Minority Links" section on the agency's Internet page.

Numbers in ***bold italic*** refer to captions and graphs.

PICTURE CREDITS

Page:
3: Digital Vision
8–9: Mark Wilson/Getty Images
11: Tim Boyle/Getty Images
14: © OTTN Publishing
16: Library of Congress
19: Library of Congress
21: Library of Congress
22: Library of Congress
24: Library of Congress
28: Library of Congress
29: National Archives
30: Library of Congress
31: Carl Iwasaki/Time Life Pictures/Getty Images
33: Library of Congress
34–35: Don Cravens/Time Life Pictures/Getty Images
37: © OTTN Publishing
40: Library of Congress
41: © OTTN Publishing
43: Library of Congress, Library of Congress
44: Library of Congress
46: LBJ Library Photo by O.J. Rapp
47: Jack Manning/New York Times Co./Getty Images
50: Arthur Schatz/Time Life Pictures/Getty Images
54: Library of Congress
56–57: Justin Sullivan/Getty Images
59: National Archives
62: Digital Vision
64: Howard Pyle/Corbis
67: Joe Raedle/Getty Images
68: © OTTN Publishing
70: © OTTN Publishing
73: CNN via Getty Images
76: Washington Bureau/Getty Images
79: © OTTN Publishing
80: Spencer Platt/Newsmakers/Getty Images
84: © OTTN Publishing
86: LBJ Library photo by Arnold Newman
89: John F. Kennedy Library, Boston
92: Digital Vision
94: Bettmann/Corbis
96: © OTTN Publishing
99: Lara Jo Regan/Liaison/Getty Images
102: © OTTN Publishing
104–105: Will Mcintyre/Time Life Pictures/Getty Images
107: © OTTN Publishing

For almost three-quarters of a century, the **GALLUP POLL** has measured the attitudes and opinions of the American public about the major events and the most important political, social, and economic issues of the day. Founded in 1935 by Dr. George Gallup, the Gallup Poll was the world's first public opinion poll based on scientific sampling procedures. For most of its history, the Gallup Poll was sponsored by the nation's largest newspapers, which published two to four of Gallup's public opinion reports each week. Poll findings, which covered virtually every major news event and important issue facing the nation and the world, were reported in a variety of media. More recently, the poll has been conducted in partnership with CNN and USA Today. All of Gallup's findings, including many opinion trends dating back to the 1930s and 1940s, are accessible at www.gallup.com.

ALEC M. GALLUP is chairman of The Gallup Poll in the United States, and Chairman of The Gallup Organization Ltd. in Great Britain. He also serves as a director of The Gallup Organisation, Europe; Gallup China; and Gallup Hungary. He has been employed by Gallup since 1959 and has directed or played key roles in many of the company's most ambitious and innovative projects, including Gallup's 2002 "Survey of Nine Islamic Nations"; the "Global Cities Project"; the "Global Survey on Attitudes Towards AIDS"; the 25-nation "Health of The Planet Survey"; and the ongoing "Survey of Consumer Attitudes and Lifestyles in China." Mr. Gallup also oversees several annual "social audits," including "Black and White Relations in the United States," an investigation of attitudes and perceptions concerning the state of race relations, and "Survey of the Public's Attitudes Toward the Public Schools," which tracks attitudes on educational issues.

Mr. Gallup's educational background includes undergraduate work at Princeton University and the University of Iowa. He undertook graduate work in communications and journalism at Stanford University, and studied marketing and advertising research at New York University. His publications include *The Great American Success Story* (with George Gallup, Jr.; Dow Jones-Irwin, 1986), *Presidential Approval: A Source Book* (with George Edwards; Johns Hopkins University Press, 1990), *The Gallup Poll Cumulative Index: Public Opinion* 1935–1997 (Scholarly Resources, 1999), and *British Political Opinion 1937–2000: The Gallup Polls* (with Anthony King and Robert Wybrow; Politicos Publishing, 2001).

HAL MARCOVITZ has written more than 70 books for young readers. His other titles in the GALLUP MAJOR TRENDS AND EVENTS series include *Technology*, *Abortion*, *Drug and Alcohol Abuse*, and *Health Care*. He lives in Chalfont, Pennsylvania, with his wife, Gail, and daughters Ashley and Michelle, and enjoys writing fiction. He is the author of the satirical novel *Painting the White House*.